The Suppressed Sister

The Suppressed Sister

A Relationship in Novels by Nineteenth- and Twentieth-Century British Women

Amy K. Levin

Lewisburg
Bucknell University Press
London and Toronto: Associated University Presses

Associated University Presses
440 Forsgate Drive
Cranbury, NJ 08512

Associated University Presses
25 Sicilian Avenue
London WC1A 2QH, England

Associated University Presses
P.O. Box 39, Clarkson Pstl. Stn.
Mississauga, Ontario,
L5J 3X9 Canada

The paper used in this publication meets the requirements of the American National Standard for Permanence of Paper for Printed Library Materials Z39.48-1984.

Library of Congress Cataloging-in-Publication Data

Levin, Amy K., 1957–
   The suppressed sister : a relationship in novels by nineteenth- and twentieth-century British women / Amy K. Levin.
      p. cm.
   Includes bibliographical references and index.
   ISBN 0-8387-5211-X (alk. paper)
   1. English fiction—19th century—History and criticism. 2. Sisters in literature. 3. English fiction—Women authors—History and criticism. 4. English fiction—20th century—History and criticism. 5. Women and literature—Great Britain—History. I. Title.
PR868.S52L48   1993
823.009′352045—dc20   91-55127
                                                                    CIP

PRINTED IN THE UNITED STATES OF AMERICA

For Beth, of course,
and the sisters I have chosen

Contents

Acknowledgments   9

1. Introduction: Blossoms on One Stem   13
2. Jane Austen: The Sister Plots   33
3. Elizabeth Gaskell: Embroidering the Pattern   54
4. George Eliot: Superfluous Sisters   78
5. Pym, Howard, and Drabble: Revising the Sister   94
6. Conclusion: Killing the Good Sister; or, The Return of the
   Witch   119

Notes   129
Bibliography   138
Index   153

Acknowledgments

Writing this book was in many ways a maturing process for me, as I reflected not only on a series of novels, but also on feminist criticism. Most of all, however, I had to confront the sister stories of my own family; in tracing sister plots in a variety of nineteenth- and twentieth-century novels, I discovered similar stories repeating themselves across generations of Tigays and Rogoffs. In coming to an understanding of others' texts, I have come to a better understanding of my history and myself. I offer this text, then, with a dual purpose: I present it not only as a work of literary criticism, but also as a challenge for women to ask questions about themselves, their sisters by birth, and their sisters by choice.

I begin, therefore, by acknowledging all the different sisters—my biological sister, Beth; my mother and her sister, Corinne; my grand-mothers, Bertha and Jennie, and their sisters. My friend-sisters contributed insights and helpful readings from the instant I first thought of writing about sisters until I completed the manuscript. In this respect, I am particularly grateful to Suzanne Juhasz, Cindy Carlson, and Mickie Grover.

Portions of chapter 5 originally appeared in an article entitled "Borrowed Plumage" in volume 12 of *Women's Studies*. Gordon and Breach Science Publishers has given permission for the inclusion of this previously published material in *The Suppressed Sister*.

Finally, I wish to thank my three readers at the City University of New York Graduate Center. Gerhard Joseph spent many hours encouraging me to probe linguistic and psychological issues in depth, making this book what it is today. Mary Ann Caws and Rachel Brownstein read the manuscript carefully and provided detailed advice and commentary.

In the end, then, like the sisters I discuss in the following pages, this work is a collective creation.

The Suppressed Sister

1

Introduction
Blossoms on One Stem

When I was in fourth grade, my sister Beth and I received our first watches, round Timexes with a picture of Disney's Cinderella on the face. Each watch came with a china statue of Cinderella, her hair golden, her blue dress billowy. We loved her story and wished we, too, had straight blond hair.

At about the same time, my mother and her sister took us to Concord, Massachusetts, to visit Louisa May Alcott's house. They bought us a hardback copy of *Little Women* with glossy pictures;[1] little women ourselves, we read it avidly. Was I, Amy, like Amy March? Did my sister Beth share Beth March's silent goodness? As an aspiring writer, I felt more empathy for Jo than for Amy, and, therefore, the story made me uncomfortable, especially when strangers would hear our names and ask whether our other two siblings were named Jo and Meg. Alcott's novel set a standard of sisterly solidarity that I believed we could never attain, no matter how close we were, or, as Louise Bernikow has put it, "it presented me, in my childhood, an image of what I did not have."[2] Like "Cinderella," *Little Women* seemed designed to unsettle, reminding me that my life often fell short of my ideals.

From the beginning, then, stories of sisters and sisterhood have inscribed themselves on my life and marked its time. I grew up to tales of my grandmothers and their sisters; raised in a succession of foreign countries, my sister and I were thrown together for companionship. We read voraciously, anything we could find in English, and many of our favorite books were tales of sisters—Wilkie Collins's *Woman in White* and *No Name*, Jane Austen's *Pride and Prejudice*, Margaret Mitchell's *Gone with the Wind*.[3]

Several years ago, however, I was struck by an odd circumstance. On the one hand, I was reading a spate of new and reissued novels that featured sisters prominently—Antonia Byatt's *Still Life*, Rebecca West's *Fountain Overflows*, Elizabeth Gaskell's *Wives and Daughters*,

Gail Godwin's *Mother and Two Daughters* and *Odd Woman*, Marilynne Robinson's *Housekeeping*, and Alice Walker's *Color Purple*.[4] These books depicted sisters' relationships as troubling, guilt-ridden, and even overtly hostile. Focusing on women's development, these novels were accompanied by a multitude of critical texts systematically tracing every imaginable relationship among women. Literary critics covered friendships, father-daughter relationships, mother-daughter bonds, lesbian affairs—everything except sisters. They tended to present relationships among women—with the exception of the mother-daughter bond—in a more positive light than in novels about sisters. A few articles and books did deal with famous sisters' biographies; others devoted a brief space (often little more than a page or two) to sisters. Several unpublished manuscripts focused on sisters in novels, but these works failed to find satisfactory explanations for the discomfort and tension among biological sisters or to discuss the relationship in fiction in any systematic way.

A review of the literature on sisters has confirmed my initial impression. Toni McNaron's *Sister Bond* is a collection of articles, primarily about the lives of famous sisters. An article by Susan Lanser in McNaron's book draws connections between the siblings in Austen's novels and Austen's relationship with her sister Cassandra. In *Among Women*, Louise Bernikow devotes one chapter to sisters, but she, too, deals little with novels. Christine Downing's 1988 work, *Psyche's Sisters*, provides a detailed analysis of the psychology of sisters' relations and of the mythology pertaining to sisters, but it scarcely concerns itself with fictive sisters. Elizabeth Fishel's *Sisters* and Dale Atkins's *Sisters* are primarily psychological studies drawing on the lives of contemporary women. And Carol Lasser's recent article on blood sisters' ties as models for female friendship, although useful, is sociological and does not refer specifically to novels.[5]

Literary critics seem either to study the bonds between biological sisters or those between friend-sisters, but not the connections and distinctions between the two kinds of relationships. Moreover, their work often limits its scope, concentrating on one author or period, rather than seeking a pattern to sisterly relationships in fiction. Patricia Spacks's article, "Sisters," focuses on biological kin in eighteenth- and early nineteenth-century novels. Spacks introduces aspects of sisterly relationships that are found in later novels as well, including the division between a "good" woman and her sister who is morally inferior, even though the latter is more beautiful and enjoys herself more. However, Spacks does not discuss works written by later authors.[6]

In her unpublished dissertation, "Sibling Relationships in Jane

Austen's Fiction," Glenda Ann Hudson relies on plot details to illustrate blood sisters' relationships. Although she indicates the incestuous nature of the bonds between sisters and brotherly lovers and discusses the Cinderella archetype, she draws little on issues of psychology or identity. Her work appears only minimally influenced by contemporary feminism or theories of female psychology, and the differences between biological sisterhood and metaphorical sisterhood are not her central concern.[7]

In contrast, Joanne Creighton raises significant issues about psychology and character in her essay, "Sisterly Symbiosis: Margaret Drabble's *The Waterfall* and A. S. Byatt's *The Game*." Her discussion is limited to two authors, although parts of it may fruitfully be extended to other writers.[8]

Rhoda Irene Sherwood's unpublished dissertation, "'A Special Kind of Double': Sisters in British and American Fiction," contains pointed analyses of several works but fails to trace a systematic pattern in sisters' relationships, in part because she does not discriminate between novels of the nineteenth and twentieth centuries, from Britain and America, or by male and female authors.[9] While many of the texts described above tend to be narrow in scope, hers presents such a broad picture that distinctions become blurred.

The authors I have discussed maintain rigid divisions between blood and fictive kin relationships, but, more often, when literary critics talk about blood sisters, they tend to slide into a discussion of nonbiological sisterhood. Nina Auerbach's *Communities of Women* offers a prime example of the confusion in discussions of the two terms. Auerbach opens her work with the *Graie* of Greek mythology, and, although she acknowledges that they are biological kin, she soon refers to the three figures as an example of sisterhood.[10] Similarly, in her discussions of *Pride and Prejudice* and *Cranford*, Auerbach portrays the family as porous and extended; she makes little distinction between biological sisters and sisters by choice. Crucial differences in the two kinds of relationships are erased.

No doubt one source of the confusion is linguistic, because a single word, *sister*, describes two dissimilar bonds. Both words, *sister* and *sisterhood*, are metaphors, but they signify on different levels. When the word *sister* is used to describe a member of a sisterhood or a sister by choice, its meaning is more abstract than when it is used to describe a biological sister; dictionaries give the former meaning as secondary, explaining that it is a bond as or like that between biological sisters. Thus *sisterhood* is what Paul Ricoeur would call a "second order reference."[11] Other critics, including Jacques Derrida, have noted that the impulse to create such metaphors is evasive. Derrida describes metaphor as a "displacement,"[12] "marking the moment of the turn or detour" as it "also opens the wandering of the semantic." Considered from this perspective, when the word *sister* is applied to friends, it marks an absence; the term reminds us of what is not (a biological relationship) as well as of what is. "Metaphorization" thus allows meaning to slip and permits a word to have different senses in its "bottomless overdeterminability."[13] But what are writers eliding when they glide from biological sisters to friends? Why the slippage? Is it a lack of attention? Deflection? Denial? Suppression?

Feminist critics, beginning with Tillie Olsen, have insisted on the significance of women's silences.[14] This silence is no exception; it allows critics to avoid discussing the frequent friction among biological sisters that is so much at odds with ideals of sisterhood. The sources of the silence are not only linguistic, but also psychological, historical, cultural, economic, and political. Indeed, this silence threatens to become a veritable black hole, engulfing every possible field of study.

Where critics have been silent, novelists have been vocal, and I believe that these two circumstances are intimately connected. Therefore, after beginning with the critical silences, which are marks of an absence, I have concentrated on novels and their depiction of biological sisters. I hope that this study will clarify the hold of the sister bond on the female imagination, and, in doing so, reveal why it eludes critics and is so often suppressed.

Most of the novels involving sisters in the nineteenth and twentieth century are in the realist tradition and posit some congruity between their worlds and the world outside their covers (this notion of congruity may be a convention and a fiction in itself, but that is another discussion altogether). More specifically, the relationships in the novels are in some ways mimetic of those beyond their pages, and the conduct of sisters in these works is rooted in the behavior of living sisters.

The sister bond is a powerful factor in women's development, and women without sisters often describe the lack as significant. These emotions have been recorded by authors representing a variety of perspectives on women's psychology, ranging from Christine Downing, who relies on Jungian analysis, to Elizabeth Fishel, who has been influenced by family systems theory. As Hegel has indicated in his study of Antigone in *The Phenomenology of the Mind*, one may choose a friend, but one cannot choose or replace a brother. Although he assigns a certain spiritual and ethical primacy to the brother-sister relationship,[15] it is true that a sister, like a brother, cannot be selected, given away, or substituted. This circumstance gives the bond a privileged position, utterly unlike a friendship, which relies on mutual affinities. In Christina Rossetti's "Goblin Market," for example, "Tender Lizzie could not bear / To watch her sister's cankerous care / Yet not share."[16] Although Lizzie does not condone the actions that cause her sister's wasting away, she risks her life for her sibling. Lizzie never questions her duty, for the sisters are as "two blossoms on one stem."[17]

Because sisters grow from "one stem," much of the power of their relationship is inherent in the pre-Oedipal situation. A young boy's first attachment is to his mother; he begins to develop a sense of identity in distinguishing his differences from her. But a young girl first bonds to a member of the same sex—and this, as many feminist psychologists have noted, makes separation and the development of an individual identity particularly difficult. The problem of separation and sameness in difference is apparent in the sister bond, too, as Louise Bernikow has indicated:

Competition seems to be the language we use for the process of separation, seems to be the kind of activity we throw up against the desire to merge. . . . When the forces [of separation from the mother] turn lateral, the process is played out among sisters.[18]

Although psychologists including Jane Gallop and Juliet Mitchell have questioned their validity,[19] Freud's theories of female development offer a different explanation for the competition among sisters. As a girl's Oedipal attachment to her father grows, she may vent hostility and envy not only on her mother, but also on her sister, a less powerful female rival for his attentions. She may do so by attempting to be the "perfect" little woman, or, if there are no sons in the family, by becoming a kind of surrogate son.

The rivalry embedded in the process of separation from the mother cannot be detached from the history of women in Europe and America. Within the nuclear family, as it was constituted in the nineteenth century, sisters were largely redundant. The custom of primogeniture assigned differing roles to brothers; sisters participated alike in household tasks. If one married, the next youngest would take over her chores.

The identical position of sisters within the family further created a need to insist on difference. The most common way sisters defined themselves was (and still is) in opposition to each other:

The work of mutual self-definition seems typically to proceed by way of polarization that half-consciously exaggerates the perceived differences and attributes of the sisters ("I'm the brightest one, and she's the pretty one").[20]

In the nineteenth century, the need to establish difference was particularly important in the marriage market, where two sisters might be indistinguishable, bearing equal dowries. Thus, as Louise Bernikow has remarked, "what we have in common is what keeps us apart."[21]

This rivalry among sisters was supported by two factors. First, a woman, perceiving the powerlessness of other females in the household, might turn away from them. Secondly, the polarization, the "unspoken, unconscious, pact that neither sister need develop all her potential," kept women subservient and bound to the family, as each woman "depend[ed] upon the other to continue to act in certain ways."[22] To some extent, these behaviors persist today; the critics I have quoted are concerned about contemporary as well as past sisters.

In opposition to rivalry, the Victorian concept of separate spheres imposed on women an ideal of harmonious relations and calm within the home. Training manuals for young girls, such as *The Female Aegis* (1798), urged amity and kindness, warning mothers to "beware of teaching [their] . . . children to vie with each other; for it is to teach them envy and malevolence."[23] Brought up with such instructions, the "good" woman learned to suppress or conceal enmity or rivalry. Polarization assisted in this process; having assumed opposite positions, sisters had little middle ground for which to compete.

The value placed on conformity made the polarization uncomfortable and painful. A woman could (and can) look on her sister's differences as implicit criticism, "experiencing them as betrayal."[24] Thus, the politics of the nuclear family held sisters in a double bind, torn between an imperative for harmony and subtler goads towards rivalry.

Sisterhoods received equally ambiguous support. Louise Bernikow's assessment of the power of female friendship would have been even more valid a century ago: "In friendship, women do to each other what culture expects them to do for men and in that way, female friendships are subversive."[25] Specifically, male fear of women's collective power was encoded in training manuals and contemporary journalism as distaste for chattering, idle groups of women, criticism of unhealthy conditions in girls' schools, and suspicion surrounding Catholic sisterhoods. Although this fear initially undermined solidarity among women, later in the century women's sisterhoods, including church groups, the temperance movement, and nursing schools, came to be seen as extensions of the home into the social realm. As such, they were glorified. Carroll Smith-Rosenberg describes expressions of "hostility" among women as "so rare as to seem almost tabooed . . ."[26] in the United States, and the same was true in England.

Carol Lasser, who has extended Smith-Rosenberg's ground-breaking work, has documented how sisters' relationships, once idealized in the nineteenth century, fulfilled male fears, serving as a subversive model for sisterhoods. Noting that "the sororal bond [of blood siblings] could coexist in a variety of physical and emotional forms," she adds that "sorority served some women as one way of negotiating the sexual boundaries of the friendships, structuring both taboos and touches." The sisterly relationship allowed women to focus on their own gender by offering a homosocial structure, its decidedly feminine manner in opposition to "intellectual, unemotional masculine styles." Finally, in their "sentimental romanticism," female friends could yield more comfort than blood sisters, and thus sisterhoods threatened the male-dominated family.[27]

In this century, the messages have been less mixed. Although the nuclear family has declined, women's groups have gained strength. Even as the divorce rate has soared, women's associations, ranging from the National Organization for Women, with thousands of members, to clusters of women meeting regularly in small towns, have gained prominence and respect as political forces. In fact, it appears that the focus on harmony in sisterhoods may have been purchased at the expense of peace in the biological family. Novels concerning sisters have grown increasingly negative. In early nineteenth-century novels, a woman is rarely able to maintain a close sisterhood if she does not have harmonious relationships at home. Later, sisters come to represent the prison of society and conventions regarding female behavior; sisterhoods, or metaphorical sisters, are associated with women's development into distinct personalities. Susie Orbach and Luise Eichenbaum's assessment of the situation is accurate, for sisters, instead of serving as models of closeness, become the repositories of hostility suppressed in friendships:

> The recent delight and recognition of the importance of women's relationships and the ideology of "sisterhood is powerful" has, in some ways, served to obscure much of the pain in women's friendships.[28]

I would be greatly oversimplifying if I were to limit myself to mimetic assumptions about the connection between the characters of fiction and "real life." The use of sisters in novels serves certain purely literary functions as well, the most obvious one being that sisters generate plot. Dale Atkins has noted that "women seem to want to talk about their relationship with their sister"[29] regardless of whether the bond is happy or unhappy. I, too, have noticed that the merest mention of the topic of this work to a woman with a sister would prompt long stories of her childhood, recent experiences, arguments, and joys. Women with several sisters tended to concentrate intensely on one sibling, with this coupling becoming the focus of tremendous intimacy or furious battles for separation. At first, I thought this interest was merely due to the primacy of the bond. However, as I read and listened, it became clear that something in the nature of the relationship (with an only sister or an especially significant one) provoked narrative in much the same way as Tony Tanner has indicated that adultery generates plot.[30]

Like an adulterous woman, a significant sister subverts the social order by creating an excess, a duplication for which there is no place. When sisters compete for a lover, the resulting triangle is a mirror image of the adulterous triangle (while Tanner refers primarily to two men loving the same woman, here, two females pursue the same male). More than that, the existence of sisters generates tension as the reader seeks to understand how something can be at once similar and different. In other words, sisters create the kind of suspense and delayed gratification aroused by narrative repetition.

Furthermore, the polarization that occurs in families is often employed as a subversive narrative strategy by female authors. Each sister is assigned a role or set of personality traits; her character is a fragmented part of a whole that is rent with conflicts. Through a pair of opposite sisters, "a special kind of double,"[31] an author can thus enact an inner struggle. One sister is frequently designated as the conventional one, and the other as a rebel, permitting the author to satisfy and undermine conventions within the same text.

In *Pride and Prejudice*, for instance, Austen usually focuses on only two of the sisters at a time. She plays the passive sufferings of Jane against Elizabeth's rebellious energy and contrasts Lydia's persistent tactlessness with Elizabeth's pride. At the same time, Austen implies that these apparent opposites are inseparable; the sisters depend on each other for their self-definition. Even though Elizabeth has often been embarrassed by Lydia, she ultimately defends her sister, rebutting Lady Catherine's contention that Lydia is an unsuitable relation for Darcy. In protecting Lydia, Elizabeth is accepting not only her blood kinship but also a spiritual affinity. Elizabeth's resistance to the authority of a social superior is merely a more justifiable form of Lydia's audacious rudeness. Thus, an irony of Austen's text and other sister stories is that despite (or because of) the meticulous role splitting, sisters are inextricably linked. This conception of character is closest to Hélène Cixous's view that the notion of a unified character is essentially a convention, and that " 'I' is more than one."[32] By extension, various stances toward convention coexist in the same text.

The fragmented characterization apparent in novels about sisters causes the reader to internalize certain conflicts. Robert Highbie and others have commented on how often "the protagonist functions as a transformation or replacement for our 'I,' "[33] and Adrienne Rich has suggested that a woman might participate especially in this process, seeking "guides, maps, and possessions. . . ." Yet the reader of a novel with a single female protagonist may feel disappointment when "over and over . . . she comes up against something that negates everything she is about: she meets the image of woman in books written for men."[34] In novels about sisters, however, the reader is presented with two or more protagonists and forced to side with one of them. The reader must then participate in a struggle for detachment from the other sister(s) in the text, and, in doing so, question her own values. In the process, she may find the woman who embodies her deepest-held desires for female solidarity. Indeed, she may discover a metaphorical sister (and, ultimately, much of the confusion between sisters and sisterhood may arise at this moment of identification).

Writers are readers as well. This fact is particularly evident in twentieth-century sister stories, where authors react to their predecessors (and their fictional characters) as sisters in addition to depicting sisters in their novels. Their fictions revise earlier female stories, even as they question patriarchal conventions. A novel may then be a gesture against the oppressiveness of two conventions, one female and one male. In *The Fountain Overflows,* for instance, the heroine feels trapped in a plot over which she has no control:

> Also I realized that a drama about me and my family had been composed by someone and had for some time been in the course of performance, and it would be no use for me to walk on the stage and protest that the truth had been perverted, for every member of the audience had had his mind made up for him by what he had already heard.[35]

Although Rebecca West's heroine is a character in a story, she expresses a feeling of entrapment in the family and pre-existing plots with which many writers can identify. Alienation is caused not only by the plots themselves, but also by the prejudices of the audience, which she describes as masculine and close-minded.

Indeed, sister stories by female authors are based on male fictions, perhaps the most significant of which are the tales of Cinderella and Psyche. Other important narratives include those of Antigone, Beauty and the Beast, Snow White and Rose Red, and King Lear. These traditional plots prepare for and support the role splitting found in nineteenth-century families and theories of female psychology. In *The Uses of Enchantment,* his study of European fairy tales, Bruno Bettleheim has found this division again and again, concluding that "polarization . . . dominates fairy tales."[36] Even in the story of Snow White and Rose Red, the only positive portrait of sisters, the siblings are depicted as being essentially opposite, not only in appearance but also in behavior. Resembling sisters in other tales, these sisters must disagree before they can marry happily. As Elizabeth Fishel comments, "Like Mary and Martha, they, too, represent the two paths, the seeker and the stay-at-home, the wanderer from home and mother and the mother's helper, her psychic extension."[37] The sisters in this fairy tale are complementary; they achieve happiness because they do not compete, and, miraculously, the twin of one sister's beloved appears to marry her sibling.[38]

"Snow White and Rose Red" is not one of the most famous sister stories. Better known sister stories "normally endorse enmity between women, who become rivals for the father's approval,"[39] and in repeating themselves, they create a pattern. This pattern owes something to fairy tales' three brothers motif, in which three siblings are tested, and the youngest, the one who initially seems least likely to prosper, succeeds. However, it is not identical to the three brothers configuration, for the overt goal of the competition among women is the love of their father or a suitor, although the real struggle is in fact for self-determination. While the male hero's quest takes him on a journey, as Nina Auerbach has shown, the female quest is essentially spiritual and internal. Instead of voyaging into the world, the heroine searches for "rootedness" and home,[40] confronting not strangers but sisters who are in effect parts of herself.

The myth of Psyche is a paradigm of the female quest, even as it illustrates the traditional suppression of the sister story in favor of a plot that favors heterosexual love. Until this century, the myth was regarded almost entirely as a romantic story (in his "Ode to Psyche," for instance, Keats does not mention the heroine's sisters). Erich Neumann's great contribution to the study of this myth is his realization that "the sisters represent an aspect of the female consciousness that determines Psyche's whole subsequent development. . . ."[41] Indeed, Neumann's analysis has been instrumental in the reappropriation of the myth by feminist critics, whether or not they agree with his reading of it.

In the myth of Psyche, marriage divides the heroine from her sisters. According to Neumann's translation, the sisters initially grieve at the loss of their sister,[42] as if they have lost part of themselves (and indeed they have). It is only when they are reunited with Psyche at the latter's request that their envy and hostility become overwhelming. Difference is the source of this envy; if Psyche's life were exactly like theirs, they would see no need for rivalry. Thus, the original female dilemma of sameness and difference generates this plot, and when Psyche's sisters seek to render her unhappy, they are trying to make her resemble them, to demolish dissimilarities. Their behavior illustrates how an essential desire for closeness, a longing to merge, exists in opposition to the need for separation.[43]

Neumann makes it clear that the sisters, in urging Psyche to "break the taboo,"[44] are not entirely a malicious influence. They are engaged in the essentially masculine act of seduction and attempting to force their sister to look clearly (literally and figuratively) at her spouse. Carolyn Heilbrun's assertion that the sisters are "a force of liberation" is indeed correct.[45]

The next section of the story is paradigmatic, too, as Psyche must confront Aphrodite, the angry mother, and complete her tasks. As Neumann and others have commented, the chores involve Psyche's coming to terms with her female nature, and all are significant, especially the sorting task, a sifting of her priorities and qualities. Psyche can only complete these labors with the assistance of natural forces. She is allowed to regain her husband and join the gods through divine intervention; ultimately, the myth tells us that a woman cannot capture love through her own agencies or without banishing her sisters.

In fact, few critics have considered the implications of the sisters' deaths. Psyche is forced by the angry gods to mislead her siblings, causing their fatal accidents. Psyche is once again betraying herself by acting as a male mouthpiece. The myth suggests that in saying what is untrue to her nature a woman destroys her sisters; she cannot have both a lover and her female siblings. Further, the story implies that women must be punished for using behaviors traditionally reserved for men, such as verbal seduction and open expressions of hostility. The deaths of Psyche's sisters leave Psyche as the exemplar and expression of feminine behavior, and she relies on a male to fulfill her. The sister plot—and the sisters' plot—are extinguished so that heterosexual romance may flourish.

The story of Cinderella repeats many elements of the Psyche myth, beginning with the envious sisters. Here, the siblings are disowned and distanced as stepsisters. The Oedipal aspect of the tale is partly suppressed as Cinderella's pain is attributed to her stepsisters instead of to her stepmother.[46] In the process, Cinderella's powerful father becomes a blank, shadowy figure, rather than the locus of anger.

Like Psyche, Cinderella must come to terms with a cruel mother and sisters and participate in a sorting task by the hearth before she can marry. Moreover, as in the story of Psyche, the aggressive, domineering sisters affect traditionally male behaviors and attempt to block the concluding marriage. In Perreault's version of the fairy tale, they must therefore be destroyed, their eyes picked out and toes cut off in a "symbolic self-castration to prove their femininity. . . ."[47] The friendly godmother, who assists the heroine, fades out, unnecessary after the wedding. And, as Jack Zipes notes in his analysis of the Grimm version of the story, Cinderella undergoes her most complete transformation, from an "active" young woman into a passive "girl . . . who must obediently wait to be rescued by a male."[48] Heterosexual relations in the story obviate the need for sisterhood and reveal "how strongly male fantasizing about women and power are still entrenched in the fairy-tale genre."[49]

The pattern recurs. Part of it is found in *King Lear*, where the heroine does not succeed in defeating her sisters' machinations. By causing Cordelia's exile, Goneril and Regan initially liberate her from Lear's paralyzing control; however, unlike Psyche, Cordelia fails to survive her self-assertion. The fates of Goneril and Regan signify the destruction of masculine women, but Shakespeare does not provide a fairy-tale happy ending for his heroine.

Antigone's story provides an intriguing variation on the standard pattern, for in this myth the heroine herself suppresses or denies her sister. Readings of this myth from Hegel's on have concentrated on the story as one of a brother and sister, and while the brother-sister bond is central, the opposition between Antigone and Ismene is also revealing. As Marianne Hirsch notes, Antigone's action "is both a form of rebellion and a form of extinction."[50] When Antigone revolts against the marriage convention, the act that defines her destroys her. Yet is Ismene's choice one of continuity? Or is her married life merely another form of extinction? The myth provides no clear answer to these questions, which recur in slightly different forms in such novels as *Middlemarch*. It does, however, underscore the way patriarchal tales of sisters sacrifice closeness among women to intimacy between men and women:

Antigone ends up denying to Ismene the very sense of irrevocable kinship that motivates her to bury Polyneices. Her sense of drastic estrangement leads her to betray, with respect to her sister, the very heart of her own deepest convictions. The one so intensely pulled toward human interfusion becomes the most solitary. . . .[51]

This paradox at the heart of the myth, which has so often been ignored, leads one to wonder whether Antigone would have sacrificed herself had Ismene, a powerless woman, been the one whose life was at stake.

Other tales of sisters, including "Beauty and the Beast," which is essentially a retelling of the Psyche story, incorporate many of the same elements. I have isolated a basic plot, which, for the sake of convenience, I will call the sister plot or sister story, and which is integral to the understanding of sisterly relationships in novels by women.

Within the plot, sisters attempt to resolve the conflicting pressures from society by maintaining a surface of amiability. By the time a reader is introduced to a fictive household of sisters, childhood squabbles have been outgrown (the picture of Austen's Bennet sisters fighting over a toy is ludicrous, to say the least). Thus, the author's very choice of a time to begin the novel, the temporal frame, serves to suppress competition by emphasizing polarization. When the sisters are adolescents and the novelists begin their stories, the girls have assumed rigidly separate identities with parental encouragement. They appear to have little or no common ground over which to compete. An example of this separation is Austen's careful splitting of qualities among three of the Bennet sisters: Jane is characterized by modesty and good manners, Elizabeth by liveliness and forthrightness, Lydia by flightiness and poor taste. Austen usually focuses on two of these sisters at a time, drawing on Kitty and Mary primarily for added humor.

Although intended to circumvent competition, role splitting itself becomes a major source of tension. A repressed desire for intimacy resurfaces in efforts to make a sister identical to one's self, and sisters, powerless elsewhere, try to control their siblings. Young sisters, who often live in small communities like the town of Cranford, are surrounded by much gossip and attention. They begin to exert power among themselves, mimicking the behavior of those around them. This petty tyranny goes well beyond the normal squabbling of children, as it extends into the sisters' adolescence and undermines their romantic pursuits. For instance, in the first chapter of *Middlemarch*, Celia and Dorothea Brooke quarrel over their mother's jewels. Encoded in the argument is each sister's wish to prove herself superior by disparaging her sibling. Thus, the relationship between sisters internalizes the educative behavior of those in the surrounding society, together with its restrictions. Celia and Dorothea have no doubt experienced similar criticism from the village chorus of women, including Mrs. Cadwallader and the devout Mrs. Bulstrode.

Versions of such behavior between sisters may be found in other novels, including *Mansfield Park*, where Fanny Price gently undertakes the training of her sister Susan, and *Cranford*, where the elder Miss Jenkyns is constantly correcting Miss Matty. The instructions are not merely an assertion of power; they also suggest that the sisters are insecure about their roles and want their siblings to imitate and accept them. The sister who claims to be proudest of her differences may, in fact, feel most embattled. Ultimately then, an effort to force conformity exists in opposition to the splintering impulse, and the contradiction itself is a force that generates plot.

In many novels, this critical behavior is counteracted when one sister allies herself with the father (or a father figure), assuming his power. She is often the sister who least submits to the prescribed "woman's sphere." For instance, Austen's Emma Woodhouse, who attempts to rule the women around her, finds her sister's maternal and conjugal behavior tiresome. In contrast, her devotion to her father gives her social status as well as a rationale for not marrying. Similarly, Mrs. Bennet notes quite correctly that Mr. Bennet favors Elizabeth. The alliance with the father splits the sisters socially and spatially; one is aligned with the realm of the study, the others live in the kitchen and the parlor.

An alignment with the father figure, however, has its costs. The bond separates one sister from the world of women, removing her from their "sphere" (be it the realm of fashion and dancing, or of the kitchen). And even though the alliance may give her power over other women, it also prolongs and enforces the young woman's subordination to her father. In Gaskell's *Wives and Daughters*, for instance, Molly Gibson's dependence on her father and distress at his remarriage has incestuous undertones.

As one sister delays her entry into the world, she endangers her relationship with suitors. Emma Woodhouse nearly loses Knightley, and in other, similar cases the young woman risks losing her lover to a sister. In *Wives and Daughters*, Molly comes close to surrendering Roger Hamley to her stepsister, Cynthia.

At this point in the sister plot, role divisions break down, and relationships are most fluid. In *Sense and Sensibility*, Austen casts doubt on which sister will marry Colonel Brandon; Elizabeth Bennet is attracted to Wickham; Sir James Chettam first courts Dorothea Brooke; Henry Crawford flirts with both Bertram sisters as well as with Fanny Price. Splitting has failed to eliminate competition, and the sisters' interchangeability underscores their redundancy in the marriage market. Several narrative resolutions are conjured at once.

The sisters themselves are unable to perceive men's roles distinctly; the sister who allies herself with the father often mistakes her lover for a brotherly figure. In *Mansfield Park*, Fanny becomes Sir Thomas Bertram's protégée and perceives Edmund as a brother, as dearly loved as her blood brother, William. Molly Gibson views Roger Hamley as a sibling, and, indeed, he nearly becomes her brother-in-law. Knightley, as Emma's brother-in-law, even stands in a fraternal relation to her. In viewing a lover as a brother, the heroine may painfully conceal her affection from herself or others. Her self-negation may show itself physically, as in Molly Gibson's ill health in the last part of *Wives and Daughters*.

Corresponding to the fluidity in roles and identity, loans and transfers of clothes or other items, such as Mary Crawford's necklace in *Mansfield Park*, become fraught with tension. The heroine must undertake a sorting task not unlike Cinderella's or Psyche's, a task that involves deciding whom to trust. She must learn to recognize false suitors, such as Frank Churchill or Henry Crawford. This sifting may bring many solitary nights of introspection by the hearth.

If the sisters succeed in disentangling the knots of their lives (in such novels as *Cranford*, they fail), if the marriage plot works out to its conclusion, the sister pattern, too, settles into a different configuration. Marriage reinforces divisions, but less in terms of personality than of class and geography. Just as Cinderella becomes a princess and Psyche a goddess, Elizabeth and Jane Bennet move in different circles from Lydia, Kitty, and Mary. In *Middlemarch*, the Chettams initially have little converse with the Ladislaws. Once the splitting attains a social dimension, the sisters can put aside their personal competition, allowing greater amity to exist. Each has a life of her own.

Such endings are intriguing because the relationship between sisters is presented as if it had been entirely harmonious all along, and devoid of competition. At the end of *Sense and Sensibility*, for example, Austen writes as if only the men needed to be brought together. Similarly, the narrator comments at the end of *Middlemarch* that, "where women love each other, men learn to smother their mutual dislike."[52] Thus, at the conclusions of the novels, as in the story of Psyche, the entire pattern is erased as if it had never existed, and the relationship between women is made to fit the ideal of the sympathetic "angel in the house," devoted to all.

An alternative resolution is occasionally present in the life of an aunt (or aunts), never fully separated from the heroine's mother, despite marriage, motherhood, and changed social conditions. Aunts in such works as *Mansfield Park* or *The Mill on the Floss* replace Aphrodite or Cinderella's cruel stepmother;[53] they represent female anger, whether passive, like Lady Bertram's, or active, like Aunt Norris's. In turning against her aunts, the heroine rejects these emotions. In other texts, such as *Mary Barton* or Marilynne Robinson's *Housekeeping*, the aunt represents unconventional but more positive traits that are repressed in the heroine's home or community. Only when these traits are accepted and integrated can the heroine be happy.

In *Pride and Prejudice*, Lady Catherine, though Darcy's aunt (and eventually Elizabeth's by marriage), plays an aunt's role in the heroine's story. As Sandra Gilbert and Susan Gubar have indicated, Lady Catherine shares many of Elizabeth's traits. Her willingness to exhibit her anger is ultimately positive for Elizabeth, forcing her to confront and acknowledge her attraction to Darcy. Although Lady Catherine does not authorize the marriage, she is its "author."[54]

In this book, I plan to trace not only this pattern, but also significant deviations and developments from it. My intention is not to force novels in their richness and complexity into a rigid mold, but rather to use the pattern as a starting point. I have chosen to focus on three nineteenth-century British women writers: Austen, Gaskell, and Eliot. Although a number of other important nineteenth-century women wrote about sisters, including Harriet Martineau in *Deerbrook*, Christina Rossetti in "Goblin Market," and Charlotte Brontë in *Jane Eyre*, I have not discussed their work at length.[55] Many of these writers do not repeatedly turn to issues concerning biological sisters, or they include sisters only as marginal figures, as in *Jane Eyre*. It is tempting to discuss works by certain authors because of the importance of sisters in their own lives, but this biographical circumstance is often inversely related to the appearance of sisters in their novels. For instance, although *Villette* and *Shirley* offer fascinating portraits of sisterhood,[56] Brontë's work as a whole is most intriguing in its lack of biological sisters. This is another kind of suppression of the sister bond, where a blood sibling—specifically, Emily in *Shirley*—is distanced and turned into an unrelated friend. Charlotte Brontë (like Virginia Woolf) stands as evidence that an author's closeness to her own siblings will not necessarily lead her to write about biological sisters, as numerous critics of Austen's novels have assumed to be the case. Instead, it appears that sister bonds are so intense that women authors may feel compelled to transform or distance them. Perhaps, too, to the extent that sisters represent splintered parts of a self, the authors are rejecting those qualities and defending the identities they have carved out for themselves.

I have therefore consistently attempted to distinguish between biographical and fictive circumstances. I have selected Austen, Gaskell, and Eliot, not because of their own experiences as sisters, but because each has concentrated on the destiny of biological sisters in several texts.

In selecting texts, I have decided not to discuss a number of relevant American novels, including *Little Women* and *Gone with the Wind*. Both books would have enhanced my analysis of the sister plot, but I felt that my inclusion of American authors might flatten distinctions between national literatures, a risk I was reluctant to take.

Moreover, I have omitted from discussion several interesting sister stories by men, most notably two by Wilkie Collins, *No Name* and *The Woman in White*, as well as George Gissing's *Odd Women* (revised in this century by the American author Gail Godwin as *The Odd Woman*). Gissing's novel explores the relationship between sisters and sisterhoods, showing the dangers inherent in sisterhood.[57] Although he assigns varied roles to the Madden siblings, the women do not really develop or change, nor does their relationship. Collins's stories include blank or "unnamed" sisters—women without a social position because of their illegitimacy. Their lack of name or place in the patriarchy makes them potentially dangerous and frightening as they act out their conventional sisters' rebellious instincts. Again, though, the women are essentially static; they are not working out an identity through or in opposition to each other. A final dimension is missing in the texts by men; obviously, these works do not exemplify the relationship of a woman author to her characters as she plots questions of identity and convention. Nor can they model her confrontation with the difference between biological sisters and the ideal of sisterhood. In contrast, Austen, Eliot, and Gaskell repeatedly confront these issues. Moreover, their novels, spanning the century, display change and adaptation in the sister plot.

Because Austen's novels, especially *Pride and Prejudice, Sense and Sensibility,* and *Persuasion,* are closest to the paradigm I have set forth, they are particularly useful in tracing the specific qualities and ramifications of the pattern. *Mansfield Park* and *Emma* will be discussed, too, although in less depth. The sisters in these novels ultimately resolve their hostility, but only by entrenching differences through class and geography. Significantly, they are not able to maintain a sisterhood while single, although in several of the novels Austen implies that they will have greater success once they marry.

Gaskell's *Mary Barton, Cranford, Wives and Daughters,* and *The Life of Charlotte Brontë* are important variations on the sister story and illustrate the dangers of never leaving the hearth. The heroine in *Mary Barton* is sisterless, but her aunt is significant because she represents sexuality, which has been repressed and banished from Mary's family. In *Wives and Daughters*, Gaskell revises the Cinderella story so that the heroine nearly loses the "prince," and she raises questions about the difference between blood sisters and stepsisters. In *Cranford*, the marriage quest does not succeed, and the sisters never completely separate; they are surrounded by a subversive sisterhood that enables them to maintain domestic peace at the expense of emotional growth.

In *The Life of Charlotte Brontë*, Gaskell treats sisters and sisterhood on a different level. She adapts the life of her friend, Charlotte Brontë, to the demands and boundaries of the sister plot. In doing so, Gaskell asserts her sisterhood with another; the biography suggests that our chosen sisters, like blood sisters, are, above all, our creations, and she helps establish a "myth of devotion"[58] to distinguish between the two levels of metaphor, sisterhood and biological kinship. The promotion of this "myth of devotion," which has been popular among feminists, has resulted in a critical neglect of contending myths and stories based on sisterly competition. Gaskell's biography thus serves as a model for the suppression of sister stories in the twentieth century, as critics, seeking kinship with earlier writers, glorify sisterhood.

In Gaskell's works, hostility between sisters is more apparent than in Austen's novels; in Eliot's *Mill on the Floss, Middlemarch,* and *Daniel Deronda,* the conventions of sisterly behavior are even more stifling and inhibiting. In addition, sisters are less important in Eliot's works than in Austen's or Gaskell's novels. In *Daniel Deronda,* for instance, they hardly seem to matter at all in the plot, although their presence is crucial in the definition of Gwendolen's character. In *Middlemarch,* the distancing among sisters parallels the heroine's growing detachment from other women and society as a whole. Finally, instead of viewing role splitting as an accommodation or survival tactic, Eliot emphasizes its dangers. For her, the sister plot is inadequate because it creates differences where few or none exist; she understands that it leads to an illusory, because partial, view of the self. To grow, a woman must renounce competition and accept her similarities to as well as differences from other women.

Ultimately, women's stories about sisters may be perceived as revisions of each other—comments on a women's tradition as well as on the male conventions and female psychology behind the sister plot. This quality is most apparent in recent fiction on biological sisters, including Margaret Drabble's *Summer Bird-Cage,* Elizabeth Jane Howard's *After Julius,* and Barbara Pym's *Some Tame Gazelle* and *An Unsuitable Attachment.* These works confirm Nancy Miller's assertion about the intertextuality of women's novels: "The plots of women's literature . . . are about the plots of literature itself, about the constraints the maxim places on rendering a female life in fiction."[59] The heroines in these twentieth-century works (who often bear the names of their predecessors) feel themselves deficient because they cannot live up to an ideal of sisterly behavior inherited from a male-dominated society and women's novels. Their desire for closeness, which is consistent with this ideal, exists in opposition to a need to separate. Thus crippled by their interdependence and fractured identities, the sisters are inhibited by conventions in their relations with men and other women. Each of these authors achieves a partial solution to this impasse, but their novels' conclusions are ambiguous about the possibility of achieving sisterhood.

In the conclusion, I will take up a radically different approach to the convention in Emma Tennant's 1978 novel, *The Bad Sister*. Tennant exposes much of what is suppressed in the sister plot; by making her novel surrealistic and using shifts in time and voice, she illustrates the destructive intertwining of sisters' personalities. Tennant's revision of Sir Walter Scott's historical novel involving sisters, *The Heart of Midlothian*, also alludes to primal fears that sisterhoods consist of madwomen or witches. The text is completely slippery: one moment the sisterhood is a commune in modern London, and the heroine kills her half sister; the next, she belongs to a coven of witches, and her sister is a shadow of herself. Tennant keeps all the distinctions and role divisions fluid, and in doing so she finally "kills" the bad sister. Or does she?

My goal has been to return to the disparity in visions of sisters and sisterhood and to the difficulty in resolving it. Study of various novels of the nineteenth and twentieth centuries suggests that the terms *sister* and *sisterhood* cannot fully comprehend the possibilities for meaning contained in them; in a Derridean sense, they are overdetermined. The term *sister* can describe biological as well as emotional kinship, and the biological relationship may contain none of the affinities of the emotional bond. In essence, the word has come to stand for almost opposite relationships. Christine Downing, who has studied the effects of the mythology of sisters, has noticed the dangers of an emphasis on metaphor:

> Although feminism made us all newly aware of the importance of sisterhood, there was early on a tendency to conceive the sister bond only metaphorically and thus in high idealized terms. Almost inevitably we then found ourselves subject to intense feelings of disillusionment when our "sisters" failed us. . . .[60]

The twentieth-century novels I will discuss bring this issue to the forefront and attempt to redefine the terms *sister* and *sisterhood;* earlier, Jane Austen and her peers trace the development of the contradictory definitions, an opposition not unlike the polarities in sisters' roles. To understand the linguistic problem facing contemporary women, we must therefore address nineteenth-century fictions and their elaborate depictions of the interplay among sisters. These are the plots which have shaped us; they form our bindings, our covers.

2

Jane Austen
The Sister Plots

I *have* lost such a treasure, such a Sister, such a friend as never can have been surpassed,—she was the sun of my life, the gilder of every pleasure, the soother of every sorrow, I had not a thought concealed from her, & it is as if I had lost a part of myself. I loved her only too well, not better than she had deserved, but I am conscious that my affection for her made me sometimes unjust and negligent of others.[1]

Cassandra Austen's words on her sister's death have set the tone for much discussion of Jane Austen, creating a picture of the sisters' devotion that has spilled over into criticism of Austen's novels. Susan Lanser, for instance, claims that "a good woman, for Austen, is invariably a good sister, and a woman's defects are often signaled by her lack of sisterly concern."[2] Yet far more striking, and increasingly evident to the reader of Austen criticism, is the disparity between the harmonious relationship Cassandra describes and the hurtful bonds so often present in Jane Austen's novels. Contrary to Lanser's assertions, in Austen's novels "good" women frequently fail to live up to ideals of sisterly relations. Elizabeth Bennet suppresses the truth of Wickham's character with disastrous results for Lydia, and Marianne Dashwood becomes so engrossed in her own griefs that she ignores her sister's sorrows. Although Lanser's statement ultimately raises the question of what constitutes a "good" woman, it does not resolve the disparity between the visions of sisters evoked in Austen novels and biographies.

My intent is not to speculate on the nature of the Austen sisters' relationships or to revise biographies (although some, including Geoffrey Gorer in "Poor Honey: Some Notes on Jane Austen and her Mother,"[3] have suggested that all was not sweetness and light in the Austen home). I do not find it useful, as Glenda Ann Hudson does throughout her work, to suggest that rivalry between sisters in a particular novel might be related to Austen's chagrin at being unattached when Cassandra was engaged, or to Austen's realization that she would never marry.[4] Instead, I wish to detach the discussion of sisters in Austen's novels from her life.

Austen's books are remarkable in the way they work and rework the elements of the traditional sister plot, shaping it in a manner that has influenced later authors. In Austen's novels, sisters are not merely used as parts of plot, as a way to comment on the social status of women, or as a narrative technique for establishing character through contrast. They often become the locus of what is repressed or displaced from the marriage plot. Cassandra's description of her life with Jane is ultimately useful not because it creates a model for sisterly behavior in novels but because it provides the key terms of the dialogue on (and between) sisters: "friend," "concealment," "part of myself," and "others."

A review of Austen's works immediately reveals the prominence of sisters. In the juvenilia, sisters appear in *Lesley Castle* and *The Three Sisters;* they play parts in the incomplete novels, *The Watsons* and *Sanditon*, too. In *Northanger Abbey*, both Catherine Morland and Isabella Thorpe have female siblings, although they are unimportant in the novel. The number of sisters is most noticeable in the other five major books, and three of these works, *Sense and Sensibility, Pride and Prejudice*, and *Persuasion*, will form the main focus of this chapter. In *Sense and Sensibility*, the heroines, Elinor and Marianne Dashwood, are set off by Mrs. Palmer and Lady Middleton as well as by the Steeles. *Pride and Prejudice* includes the Bennet girls; Miss Bingley and her sister, Mrs. Hurst; the Lucas sisters; and Mrs. Bennet and her sister, Mrs. Philips. In *Persuasion*, Austen portrays the three Elliott siblings and their counterparts, the two Musgrove girls. Sisters are less important in *Emma* and *Mansfield Park* (where most of the interactions among female siblings involve secondary characters—the Bertram sisters, Fanny's mother and Fanny's aunts), and, therefore, these two novels will be treated in less depth than *Persuasion, Pride and Prejudice*, and *Sense and Sensibility*.

Embedded in the stories of these very different sisters are episodes of pain, mortification, and even hostility. The discomfort ranges from the open competition of the Bertram girls to the quiet shame of Anne Elliott at her sisters' snobbery, from the Musgrove girls' friendly rivalry for Captain Wentworth to Emma Watson's amazement at "treachery between sisters!"[5] And while Emma Woodhouse might anticipate Isabella's visit in spite of her sister's silly hypochondria, in the youthful novella *Lesley Castle*, Charlotte Lutterell's reaction to the death of her sister's fiancé is ridiculous:

Imagine how great the Disappointment must be to me, when you consider that after having laboured by both Night and Day, in order to get the wedding dinner ready by the time appointed, after having roasted Beef, broiled Mutton, and Stewed Soup enough to last the new-married Couple through the Honey-moon, I had the mortification of finding that I had been Roasting, Broiling, and Stewing both the Meat and Myself to no purpose.[6]

These examples, which are only a few of many, support Nina Auerbach's assertion that Austen's characters often "lead a purgatorial existence together," as well as Patricia Beer's conviction that Austen's heroines exhibit little "solidarity."[7]

Austen's depiction of the complex interactions among sisters engages her readers from the earliest texts. Charlotte Lutterell's dismay at her sister's cancelled engagement is broadly parodic; at the same time, it reveals how sisters depend on each other. Charlotte has derived satisfaction from planning and preparing the perfect bridal repast, and she accepts her sister's loss as her own. In *The Three Sisters*, too, Austen makes fun of sisterly behavior, as the girls engage in playful negotiations over an especially obnoxious suitor. Mr. Watts, who aspires to the hand of the eldest, sees the girls as interchangeable commodities: "If she does not choose to accept my hand, I can offer it else where . . . it is equally the same to me which I marry of the three."[8] But the three sisters do not accept the arrangement passively. They argue and tease each other in a scene that prepares for the Allabys' game of cards for a husband in Samuel Butler's *Way of All Flesh*.[9]

In *Sense and Sensibility*, Austen explores the narrative possibilities for sisters more fully. Although there are three Dashwood sisters, Elinor, Marianne, and Margaret, Austen concentrates on the elder two, rejecting the fairy-tale triad. A popular reading of the text takes the sisters as foils for each other, figures standing in for "sense" and "sensibility."[10] Such analyses assume a basic separation in the two figures, while, as Tony Tanner has noted, from the title on, the two "add up to one divided self"; like Cassandra, Austen considers sisters parts of one being. One can understand Marianne best in her contrast to Elinor, and Elinor gains much of her sense of self in comparison to her sister. In short, they are "not a simple dualism. They *are* not simply ciphers for passion and reason, impulse and restraint, feeling and form, poetry and prose."[11]

Indeed, Elinor and Marianne have little opportunity to separate. In their selfish machinations to give the girls as little as possible, the John Dashwoods treat them as a unit. The meager pittance grudgingly allotted to the girls, their sister, and their mother, virtually ensures their continued togetherness, for their income is too low to be attractive in the marriage market.

In reaction to the social forces combining to treat them as duplicates in a crowded field, the girls pride themselves on their dissimilarities. These differences are exhibited in habitual patterns of behavior that create the illusion that the sisters are mere foils for one another. Elinor appears more practical than the romantic Marianne. Marianne's impetuousness makes her "resemblance . . . [to] her mother . . . strikingly great";[12] Elinor's commonsense concerns, including the family finances, align her with the world of men. She will not allow herself to indulge in Marianne's stereotypically female behaviors—tears, sighs, illness. She is instead "the counsellor of her mother" (6). Similar splitting is apparent in secondary characters; Mrs. Palmer is "good-humoured and merry" (110), while her sister Lady Middleton is cold and vapid. Although Lucy Steele is calculating, her sister's less deliberate cruelties are evidence of stupidity and superficiality.

Personal differences are so strongly ingrained that sisters form complementary parts of one being, treating their individual character traits as possessions. Contemporary psychologists Stephen Bank and Michael Kahn have observed a similar phenomenon in a clinical setting: "A determination not to become like a particular brother or sister means that one has given up certain options of behavior and has relegated them to the other sibling."[13] Bank and Kahn describe this quality as common to both sexes, but, within Austen's novel, this particular type of possessiveness is primarily female. Neither Ferrars brother has a monopoly over stupidity or weakness for Lucy Steele. John Dashwood may have arrogated for himself the right to be selfish, domineering, and snobbish, but the "determination" in his case "to give up" traits was supported by cultural and social norms. With living sisters, the decision to appropriate certain personality traits takes place in childhood; Austen and other novelists use this splitting to achieve a semblance of verisimilitude as well as to fulfill narrative or thematic goals.

In *Sense and Sensibility*, role splitting defines the Dashwood sisters' relationship. Elinor feels awkward exhibiting certain qualities because they "belong" to Marianne. When Elinor learns of Edward Ferrars's engagement to Lucy Steele, for example, she cannot express her sorrow, because "Elinor was to be the comforter of others in her own distresses no less than in theirs . . ." (261). This behavior is part of her very being. In contrast, Marianne persists in seeking comfort. The complementarity of the Dashwood sisters operates in social settings, too, as "the luxurious power to withdraw from unpleasant society is purchased for Marianne by the excess of Elinor's social martyrdom."[14]

Marianne's "luxury" is not merely detrimental to Elinor. Marianne's insistence on her sensitivity draws attention to her sibling's practicality and forbearance. Elinor, who would not appear the "martyr" without Marianne, depends on her younger sibling for her social identity. Thus, differences help to create and define a self, making it recognizable.

The sisters are bound together in a complex knot of desires and needs, their relationship moving back and forth along a continuum between identification and differentiation. The paradoxical nature of this relationship, defined by both polarization and interdependence, is perhaps best characterized by Suzanne Juhasz's observation that the girls are "locked in estrangement."[15] Even as Elinor benefits from the contrasts between her personality and Marianne's, she perceives Marianne's dissimilarity as implicit criticism. Combined with an underlying wish for integration, her insecurity kindles an urge to erase all differences. However, the sisters suppress this longing because they would have to confront their social redundancy if they acted on it. The desire remains unfulfilled; its only trace is in instructive behavior, as when Elinor "might suggest a hint of what was practicable to Marianne" (261), hoping to make her sister more similar to herself.

Austen only sketches out the connections between the sister story and the marriage plot in *Sense and Sensibility;* she reserves a fuller treatment of the theme for *Pride and Prejudice.* Having aligned Marianne with her mother and made Elinor a surrogate male in the family, Austen proceeds to show how role divisions obviate the need for open rivalry over men. The handsome, impetuous Willoughby becomes Marianne's suitor—appropriately, as she, too, is impulsive and unabashedly emotional.

Rivalry is further avoided by the sisters' modes of communicating, or, to be more accurate, by the sisters' modes of *not* communicating. Marianne is reticent about discussing Willoughby's behavior, but after she receives his cruel letter, her grief is unrestrainable. Even then her exaggerated sorrow squelches any true communication. Elinor, who has her own affliction, is incapable of responding to such naive and insensitive assertions as "happy, happy Elinor, you cannot have an idea of what I suffer" (185). As Marianne works and reworks Willoughby's treachery in her mind, her talk becomes circular and disordered: "Before breakfast was ready, they had gone through the subject again and again, with . . . the same impetuous feelings and varying opinions on Marianne's [side] as before" (201). This continual rehashing does not improve Marianne's spirits. Instead, it benefits Elinor, who derives gratification from the reminder that her sister has fallen victim to a man's inconstancy, too. Elinor also gains a sense of superiority from being her sibling's protector and confidante.

In turn, the elder sister keeps to herself the knowledge of Edward Ferrars's engagement to Lucy Steele. Her sister and mother's commiseration would only remind her that she misinterpreted Edward's behavior. This failure (for so Elinor perceives it) strikes at the core of her being, since she prides herself on her ability to judge people accurately. For her, the decision to remain silent has all the strength of "necessity" (141), specifically, for self-preservation.

Elinor's silence consists not only of an unwillingness to hurt others, but also of an impulse to shield herself. Marianne illustrates the damage talk can cause; she embarrasses Elinor by assuming that Edward's ring is woven of Elinor's hair and by hinting to Mrs. Ferrars (in front of Lucy Steele no less) that Elinor's accomplishments are superior to Miss Morton's. In contrast, Elinor's unfailing politeness to Mrs. Jennings's inquiries and Lucy Steele's importunities allows her to hide painful truths. As Susan Morgan has remarked, in this novel, "politeness is not an adequate expression of our feelings and thoughts. It really is a disguise. And that is its value. It leaves space and time for something still to be known."[16] By creating "space," silence and genteel manners counteract the cramped environment of the parental home, maintaining the distance and differences between sisters. Handwork is a mask, too. Dennis Allen points out that screens like Elinor's are designed to "obscure" and that other crafts "disguise" a "lady herself."[17]

The intricate web of silence and difference does not prevent rivalry for long. The women's essential interchangeability is reasserted when Colonel Brandon chooses to wed Marianne rather than Elinor. But marriage itself establishes rigid divisions through class and geography. The pain of personal dissimilarities is all but erased, and, at the novel's close, personal rivalry is denied:

> Between Barton and Delaford there was that constant communication which strong family affection would naturally dictate; and among the merits and happiness of Elinor and Marianne, let it not be ranked as the least considerable, that though sisters, and living almost within sight of each other, they could live without disagreement between themselves, or producing coolness between their husbands. (380)

The astute reader, who has seen the lack of communication between the Dashwood sisters, and seen family affection anything but "natural" in the novel, wonders whether Austen has forgotten what she has written or whether she is being ironic. The assertions of "family affection" are contradicted by the revealing and damning observation that Elinor and Marianne get along "*though* sisters." This reminder of past friction is supported by the relationships of secondary pairs of sisters, which remain unhappy.

In the Dashwoods' story, Austen has conceded to two conventions: the happy ending to the marriage plot and the calm surface of the equally content family. The smoothness of the closing paragraph underscores its forced quality. Austen has entered the world of romance and fairy tale, leaving the telling "though sisters" as a marker of what has been suppressed.

Indeed, throughout, the use of sisters in the plot has subtle effects on another level—the reader's. In the conclusion, Austen manages at once to bow to conventions and to remind us of what has been erased, satisfying two conflicting impulses. Earlier, role splitting involves readers in the sisterly drama of separation and individuation. Patricia Spacks's remarks about authors apply to Austen's audience as well, for sister stories enable readers "to explore opposing fantasies, to imagine the pleasures of self-indulgence as well as the rewards of self-restraint."[18] Eventually, however, readers find themselves taking sides and questioning their own values.

When the sensitive Marianne behaves selfishly, readers' sympathies are engaged on Elinor's behalf. This movement toward identification and sympathy makes it easy to ignore the fact that Elinor's attempts to be the model woman of nineteenth-century training manuals often make her look smug, just as similar efforts on Fanny Price's part in *Mansfield Park* verge on priggishness. The reader, along with Elinor, adopts common sense as a virtue, only to discover its limitations. But the participatory process is more complex than that, for, in siding with Elinor, the reader may well reject traits of her own, such as sensibility. Thus, at the novel's conclusion, the reader is reminded of the dangers of denying parts of herself, of engaging in the elaborate ritual of polarization and competition.

In *Pride and Prejudice*, Austen provides a more complicated version of the ritualized sister story, in which the household contains five daughters instead of three. The number of women allows Austen to emphasize the siblings' social replication. All five are "out" together, and, consequently, in competition with each other. As Lady Catherine de Bourgh indicates, this is not a particularly enviable situation. Although Elizabeth argues that postponing the younger girls' entry into society until their elders married "would not be very likely to promote sisterly affection or delicacy of mind" (165), Mrs. Bennet's frantic pursuit of suitors scarcely "promotes" these qualities among the sisters, either.

While the sisters occupy identical social positions and compete for recognition in the marriage market, each fills a carefully defined role in the family. Jane is quiet; Elizabeth is lively; Lydia chatters incessantly; Kitty imitates Lydia; Mary is plain and pedantic. These characterizations, though simplistic, reflect the sisters' perceptions of themselves. In fact, the sisters actually share certain emotions; for instance, Jane and Elizabeth are humiliated by their mother's schemes to find them husbands. And, although they deny being similar, both Lydia and Elizabeth display high spirits and rebellious energy.

As in *Sense and Sensibility,* divisions serve a multitude of purposes, revealing the dependence and interplay among sisters, even as they obscure the sisters' social redundancy. Moreover, here too, Austen focuses on only two of the sisters at a time, either Elizabeth and Jane or Elizabeth and Lydia. Concentration on a pair of sisters sets differences in relief so that the siblings appear diametrically opposed (even when they are not), drawing attention to the way sisters define their identities in relation to each other.

The role of "emotionally significant pairs" of siblings has been documented by Bank and Kahn, who have noticed that the relationship "can be either negative or positive, in the service of either love or hate. Each sibling appears to obtain more pain or more pleasure from one sibling to the exclusion of other children in a family."[19] Elizabeth Bennet is divided both ways; she derives support and affection from Jane, and negative self-definition from Lydia. Whenever she focuses on one of these sisters, she "excludes" the other.

Kahn and Bank have traced this bond in adolescence, where "there is no neutrality or indifference . . . a particular sibling is the one who really 'counts.'" They have found that in families like the Bennets', where there is an odd number of children, one sibling is always left out, just as Mary is excluded from the frequent pairing of Jane with Elizabeth and Kitty with Lydia.[20] The shifting alliances indicate the essential instability of the Bennet family; the fact that, in both dyads, the younger sibling is most powerful also creates tension.

Elizabeth and Lydia take particular pleasure in their differences from their elders. Elizabeth is mortified by Lydia's flamboyant flirting, and, although she feels more positively toward her elder sister, she boasts of being more discerning than Jane (ironically, this famous discernment does not permit her to see through Wickham's wiles unaided).

A fragment of a conversation between her and Jane reveals how sisterly differences allow the girls to "define themselves by studying each other, comparing and contrasting. . . ."[21] Elizabeth begins by praising Jane's tolerance extravagantly: "You are too good. Your sweetness and disinterestedness are really angelic; I do not know what to say to you." Yet Elizabeth's approving remark may have a sardonic intent, for Elizabeth, who prides herself in her careful choice of language, is usually thrifty with compliments. The subtext of Elizabeth's remark is defensive; she quickly returns to herself, condemning her own actions to elicit reassurance: "I feel as if I had never done you justice, or loved you as you deserve." Almost automatically, Jane complies: "Miss Bennet . . . threw back the praise on her sister's warm affection" (134–35). Clearly, this ritual has been performed many times; it is one of the ways in which the two support each other.

Lydia's communications also evoke an intricate game of double (though not necessarily hidden) messages. Her effusive, excessive delight at her marriage, her ostentatious move to take precedence over Jane, and her insensitive offer to find spouses for her sisters are not as ingenuous as she wishes them to appear. Lydia, "who never heard or saw anything of which she chose to be insensible" (310), thoroughly enjoys the scene; she is rubbing in the fact that she is married and thus socially superior to her single sisters.

These dialogues demonstrate how sisters constantly judge, compare, and seek reassurance from one another. But why are Lydia and Elizabeth particularly disposed to this prolonged game of one-upmanship? Elizabeth's sense of herself is founded on her superior discrimination; her personality is determined by her differences from her siblings, whom she considers representatives of conventional femininity. Lydia's behavior is no doubt in part the youngest sibling's revenge for having been last all her life. Lydia gains self-definition from her identification with her mother and other women. Her pride in her conquests and social successes is designed to strengthen that bond and to remind her siblings of their "failures" in that area.

For Lydia and Elizabeth, as for their sisters, the constant comparisons and embarrassments bring "pain" as well as "pleasure" (326). Even as Elizabeth feels mortified by Lydia's behavior, these gestures confirm her sense of self. In this way, a sister's misdeeds shape the heroine's personality as much as her own actions. This circumstance is intimately connected to the construction of personality in the text. Because the sisters are split-off parts of one self, they are in fact reacting to tendencies of their own that have been denied. A male hero will learn from travel and adventure, but these heroines remain close to home, and they are formed by forces within that frame.

The friction among sisters is augmented by the girls' competition for parental approval. A scarcity of adult love and attention accompanies the literal poverty of the Bennet household. The young women in the novel, like those Elizabeth Fishel interviewed for her book on living sisters, must compete for what little affection exists:

> The gold cup of parental love . . . is never perceived as a cup which runneth over, rather a finite vessel from which the more one sister drinks, the less is left for the others.[22]

A sense of scarcity leads to jealousy, which role splitting cannot erase. Instead of sharing, Lydia and Elizabeth must have parents of their "own."

While Elizabeth is closeted with her father or enjoying brisk walks, her mother shepherds the younger girls into town, where the participate in the rounds of female gossip, shopping, and flirting with the militiamen (Elizabeth's attraction to Wickham takes her briefly into this world, but her final choice of the patrician Darcy reinforces an alliance with her father to the exclusion of her mother). Lydia, Mrs. Bennet's favorite, is spoiled and forgiven everything.

Jane, who does not encourage her mother's foolishness, is not as critical of others as Elizabeth and her father tend to be. Her neutrality allows Jane the independence to begin her romance with Bingley.

Admitted to the sanctum of her father's study, Elizabeth is his acknowledged favorite and confidante: ". . . Lizzy has something more of quickness than her sisters" (5). She has inherited her father's "mixture of quick parts, sarcastic humour, reserve, and caprice" (5), which makes her mistrusted and at times disliked by other women. These feelings are mutual. She wastes no time, for instance, in noticing that Miss Bingley's behavior at its best is "all that was affectionate and insincere" (383).

In linking herself with her father, a young woman allies herself with power, which intimidates other young women. Elizabeth is comfortable with her father, but Kitty is afraid of him and does not understand his humorous threats. This alignment also conveys the privilege of being included in family secrets, as when Mr. Bennet tells his elder two daughters of Mr. Gardiner's measures to ensure Lydia's marriage. He does not think of including his wife in this confidence, and when Elizabeth and Jane suggest that Mrs. Bennet ought to know, "without raising his head, [he] coolly replied, 'Just as you please'" (305). Lizzy and Jane are left to act as intermediaries. Their ability to perform this function is an expression of their equivocal position, permitted on sufferance in the study, but returned bearing dispatches to the female realm of the kitchen. In addition, their ability to carry such important news to their mother indicates their strength in the household—and Mrs. Bennet's powerlessness.

The elements of secrecy and power give the favored daughter's relationship with her father incestuous overtones. As Elizabeth is admitted to knowledge forbidden to her mother, the distinctions between the terms *daughter* and *wife* loosen. Françoise Basch has noted how easily relationships become fluid:

> They [single women] move in a world where characters and authors frequently confuse filial, conjugal, fraternal and passionate love, sublimate passion into chaste fraternal love, convert paternal love into conjugal love.[23]

Austen is creating just such a world, not of literal incest, but of shifting boundaries and definitions concerning human relations. This confusion exists in spite of the rigid divisions among sisters.

In fact, this fluidity in heterosexual relations stems from the same roots as sisters' role divisions. The desire to assert her separateness from a sister, to be more than an undifferentiated daughter, can lead a young woman to sanction a relationship that appears to transgress boundaries. The special bond with her father removes the girl from the anonymous category of *daughter;* she begins to replace *wife.* According to James Twitchell, ordinarily, "the naming function of language" is "one of the strongest announcers and enforcers" of the incest taboo:

> The process of naming is the process of categorizing, which is the unconscious establishment of limits, in this case sexual limits. . . . In other words, the semiotics of incest—the social code—may be far more potent than the biology of inbreeding—a genetic code.[24]

But in Austen's novels, language cannot always "enforce" the taboo. The very "process of naming" is alien to sisters, who find it lumps them together.

Indeed, the "naming function of language" may illustrate and perpetuate women's social redundancy. The recurrence of women's Christian names in Austen's novels, the abundance of Janes, Annes, Fannys, and Elizabeths, underscores the fact that they duplicate each other. Women's family names are not their own, but rather markers of their social status and kinship; men, possessing both their own Christian and family names (and, like Darcy, often referred to by their family names alone), have more standing in Austen's society. Ultimately, when a woman assumes her husband's name upon marriage, the name becomes another marker of her detachment from her family. She is separated not only by class or geography, but also by language itself.

Before this resolution can occur, however, the fluidity in the "categorizing" of relationships at home must spill over into the marriage plot. Just as Elizabeth's relationship to her father has its ambiguities, her interactions with suitors are undefined. Wickham, for instance, exists in the category of *suitor* before he becomes a brother-in-law. And Darcy's actions towards Elizabeth are even more ambiguous. Although Glenda Ann Hudson holds that every suitor in Austen's works is essentially a "brotherly lover,"[25] I agree with Rachel Brownstein's contention that Darcy is a father figure. Brownstein notes that Darcy scolds and corrects Elizabeth from the beginning; his resemblance to Mr. Bennet is apparent when Darcy "admires her above all other women" and behaves in a "haughty and exigent" manner.[26]

If the men's positions are unclear, the women's roles are similarly undefined, because the sisters are interchangeable. Wickham's shifting affections best illustrate their duplication. The sisters' attempts to define themselves and each other are subverted by male expectations and assumptions; in essence, their efforts to create themselves or their own plots are undermined by a male version of romance, in which marriageable women, like daughters at home, are exchangeable and inferior. A woman, one of many in her category (and one of many bearing her name), may be redundant, but a suitor, like a father, retains his singularity.

Nevertheless, the sisters continue to struggle against their social duplication. The fluidity in heterosexual relations, together with the existence of secrets from which one or more sisters may be excluded, eventually results in reduced communication, much like the restraint between Elinor and Marianne Dashwood. Elizabeth silences herself regarding Wickham's character, not only because she is bound to secrecy, but also because she fears that Lydia would doubt her anyway (and perhaps Elizabeth wishes to remove an embarrassing irritant from the family). Jane and Elizabeth confide in each other less openly, too; conversation with or without undertones is minimal. Anger and sorrow are displaced onto the powerful, nasty, older woman, Lady Catherine de Bourgh. Because Lady Catherine is outside the family, she is a "safe" repository for otherwise inexpressible emotions. Like Aphrodite in the myth of Psyche, Lady Catherine acts as a model of female strength, at once an obstacle in the heroine's path and an enabler who forces her to come to terms with herself when her sisters are powerless.

The increased silence between the sisters is an essential part of the sister plot, because it throws the heroine closer to her suitor. Secrets, reinforced by Elizabeth's physical distance from her sisters, begin to wear her down. She starts to appreciate Darcy on her trip with the Gardiners. His solace after Lydia elopes consoles the heroine for the lack of Jane's companionship.

Another factor that brings the heroine closer to her suitor is rivalry from outside the family. None of Elizabeth's sisters competes openly with her for the "right" suitor, Mr. Darcy. Instead, Lady Catherine's officious meddling on behalf of her daughter forces Elizabeth to acknowledge her attraction to Darcy. The role splitting and lack of communication within the family have made participation in a sister's quest for a spouse almost impossible. Even when Elizabeth wants to bring Jane and Bingley back together, she is virtually helpless. Only Darcy's instigations and Miss Bingley's spite can overcome Jane's diffidence.

Once the sisters are engaged, conflict is resolved through means other than role splitting in a conclusion that resembles the end of *Sense and Sensibility*. Jane and Elizabeth are separated from the irritants in the family; once married, the two see little of Lydia, Mary and Mrs. Bennet, while Mr. Bennet is permitted to drop in unannounced. Kitty is "improved" (385) by her two eldest sisters and kept away from Lydia's noxious influence. The divisions are reinforced by class; the Darcys are social superiors to the Wickhams and thus have little occasion to mingle with them.

In *Pride and Prejudice* and *Sense and Sensibility*, Austen incorporates elements of traditional myths and fairy tales in her sister plot. Like Cinderella, Elizabeth Bennet is associated with her father and uncomfortable in the world of women; Elizabeth also shares Cinderella's exclusion from the higher ranks of society. However, the greatest resemblance between Austen's books and the stories of Cinderella and Psyche is the role splitting among sisters, which is also apparent in *Persuasion*.

Persuasion revises archetypes more radically than the other two novels. Instead of associating her heroine with the world of men, Austen places Anne in the position of the outcast youngest child. The author changes the fairy-tale three-sibling pattern, making the tested child the mother's favorite and the middle sibling (a revision that fits actual sibling patterns, since middle children often feel neglected). Finally, like Psyche, Anne has had a lover and lost him, although not so much through her sisters' influence as through the persuasion of Lady Russell, her surrogate mother and a Venus figure in the novel.

Anne is displaced within her family and within society. The pain and mortification caused by her sisters, especially Elizabeth, although

masked by a surface of calm and politeness, are severe. Whereas
Elizabeth Bennet may feel some sisterhood toward Charlotte Lucas,
for most of the novel Anne lacks contact with congenial or sensible
peers. She and Mrs. Croft are little more than acquaintances; Mrs.
Smith does not move in the same social circles or truly understand
Anne's motives. Lady Russell, when she is present, remains intimidating and peremptory.

The situation is worsened by the family's financial plight and move
to constricted quarters. As in the opening of *Sense and Sensibility,*
when John Dashwood denies his family sufficient financial support,
physical poverty is a metaphor for emotional deprivation. Sir Walter
Elliott is unable to pay attention to Anne because, if he did so, he
would be scanting Elizabeth, and, worse, himself. Instead, he views
Anne as a disposable, if useful, commodity; she is to occupy herself
quietly without demanding any attention, or she is to be thrust out of
the way. Here, too, Austen replicates the situation in *Sense and Sensibility,* where it is obvious that John Dashwood considers the heroines
unnecessary encumbrances and perpetual annoyances.

Despite such similarities, Austen's portrayal of family relations in
Persuasion is darker than in her earlier works. In *Mansfield Park* and
Sense and Sensibility, relationships among secondary sisters are inferior
to those involving the heroine and her siblings. In *Persuasion,* Anne
feels isolated in the midst of her snobbish siblings, while the secondary set of sisters, the Musgroves, get along quite well. Louisa may be
livelier and more forthright than her sister, and the two may initially
compete for Captain Wentworth, but their anger toward each other is
short-lived.

A more significant sign of Austen's pessimism is her treatment of
Anne's relationship with her father. Instead of favoring the heroine,
Sir Elliott prefers Elizabeth: "For one daughter, his eldest, he would
really have given up any thing, which he had not been very much
tempted to do."[27] Although Elizabeth is nominally mistress of the
household, she is a failure at housekeeping, and Lady Russell finds
little resemblance between the daughter and her deceased mother. On
the other hand, Anne shares her mother's managerial expertise as well
as her gentleness: "It was only in Anne that she [Lady Russell] could
imagine the mother to revive again" (6).

This shift emphasizes the negative consequences of an alliance with
the father. In the earlier novels, the heroine's closeness to her father is
often a mark of her (and his) good sense, even though the association
sets the woman apart from other females. For instance, when Elizabeth Bennet considers Mr. Collins's proposal, her father jokes that, no

matter what she decides, she will lose the affection of one parent. Elizabeth has no qualms about seeking her father's approval and not her mother's. In *Sense and Sensibility,* Elinor appears admirable for performing fatherly duties for her mother and sisters.

In *Persuasion,* however, the father's favorite inherits only his foolish snobbery. Elizabeth Elliott's vanity effectively shields her from close contact with her equals, except the obsequious Mrs. Clay, and her toadying to nobility underscores the absence of any genuine esteem between her and other females. Elizabeth's intimacy with Sir Walter Elliott, although different in character from Elizabeth Bennet's bond to her father, has a similar effect, isolating her from her gender. Whereas in the earlier novel Austen treats a woman's alliance with her father humorously and ironically, here the results appear darker.

In *Persuasion,* Austen has further manipulated the materials of the standard sister plot in stretching it temporally. In *Sense and Sensibility* and *Pride and Prejudice,* the main sisters' marriages occur within a short period of time. Here, the marriage plot is interrupted, and the results include heightened friction among the sisters and continued fluidity in family relationships. Anne and Wentworth's courtship is suspended when he sets sail, and Austen takes up and completes another marriage plot instead.

The latter story dislocates the sister pattern. Anne, having relinquished Wentworth, is stuck within the family, as if she were bound in a relationship with her father. Instead of treating Charles Musgrove as a brother and then realizing his potential as a husband, Anne turns a suitor into a fraternal figure. When Charles Musgrove proposes to Anne, she rejects him, and he "not long afterwards found a more willing mind in her younger sister . . ." (28). In addition to revealing once again how men treat women as interchangeable commodities, this sequence shows how Anne has learned from her renunciation of Wentworth. She resists Musgrove's proposals even though the influential Lady Russell "lamented her refusal . . ." (28). Years of loneliness have taught her that Lady Russell's advice is not always correct.

Anne's reflections on Musgrove's marriage reveal another significant point: she can feel envy. Her feelings toward her sister are no indicator of her moral worth, and this circumstance further contradicts Susan Lanser's assertion that sisterly behavior and "goodness" are inextricably linked in Austen's novels.[28] Indeed, despite her apparent tolerance of her sister's behavior, Anne believes that Charles might have been better off marrying a different kind of person:

A woman of real understanding might have given more consequence to his character, and more usefulness, rationality, and elegance to his habits and pursuits. (43)

Austen's initial description of Anne as having "an elegance of mind and sweetness of character, which must have placed her high with any people of real understanding . . ." (5) is echoed by this description of the ideal spouse for Charles. Yet, although Anne hints that she might have been a superior wife for Charles, she does not grieve seriously over him. Instead, she understands that a husband, like a father, can convey power and status, and, as the Cinderella of her family, she is effaced:

> Only Anne—no rank, no effective surname, no house, no location; her words are weightless, and physically speaking she has always to 'give way'—that is, accept perpetual displacement.[29]

Unmarried and unloved, Anne has no "place" of her own in society or the family. She is welcomed in neither the parlor nor the study; when the family moves, she is no more at home in Bath than on her visit to the Musgroves.

The interchangeability of sisters, while a motif in Austen's other novels, resurfaces and is especially prominent in the main plot of *Persuasion*. Musgrove's proposals in the "interim" story prepare for similar behavior on the part of the other male characters. Wentworth briefly excites competition between the Musgrove sisters when he dallies with both. Mr. Elliott, too, transfers his affections from Elizabeth to Anne. Initially, any socially appropriate woman will be acceptable to the men; a sign of Wentworth's excellence is that he comes to recognize Anne as an individual, rather than as part of a group or unit. In essence, he allows Anne her own story.

Male inconstancy increases the competition among women, contributing to the silences that pervade this most inward of Austen's novels. Such characters as Elizabeth, Mary, and Mrs. Clay may chatter incessantly, but they communicate little, and their speech ultimately has an effect similar to silence. In fact, the Elliott sisters are remarkable in their lack of understanding of each other, and Anne's restraint, like Elinor Dashwood's, is formidable. She does not discuss her attraction to Wentworth, her grief over her family's treatment of her, or her discomfort with Mr. Elliott's attentions, as she has "habitually used the minor rules of propriety to conceal her feelings and motives. . . ."[30] Anne's reserve distances her from the sisterhood of other women as well as from her family. Mrs. Smith has to base her impressions of Anne on gossip received third hand, and, as a result, she is surprised to discover Anne's distaste for Mr. Elliott. Silence, which began for Anne as a way of dealing with family, has become part of her self-effacement.

Anne's sisters hinder more than help her, and, ultimately, as with Elizabeth Bennet, competition from outside the family (Louisa Musgrove) forces her to acknowledge love. At the end of the novel, Anne goes to sea, physical distance separating her from clamorous sisters and a haughty father. Space replaces silence. Austen allows the heroine a new sister in Mrs. Admiral Croft, for Anne, having extricated herself from the family web, is able to make friends elsewhere. But even though the break from family is more complete than in *Pride and Prejudice*, Austen fails to erase tension or create harmony as in *Sense and Sensibility*. The author ultimately leaves the problem of sisters in the balance; she shows how role splitting harms siblings, but she offers no true resolution.

In *Mansfield Park* and *Emma*, siblings are less central than in the novels discussed so far, but, like *Persuasion*, both books offer ambiguous endings to the sister plot. *Mansfield Park* illustrates what happens when marriages that entrench differences nevertheless fail to banish rivalry; Aunt Norris, Mrs. Price, and Lady Bertram continue to express anger in their manipulations of each other and their families. With this model, it is little wonder that the Bertram sisters squabble perpetually (indeed, their behavior serves as an inverse example of the ideal of sisterhood). Henry Crawford's flirtation with both girls escalates their competition, which is interrupted only when they unite in tormenting Fanny.

Why do the Bertrams squabble so much more than Austen's other sisters? Aside from Aunt Norris's preference for Maria, they are neglected by their elders, and neither is aligned with a parent. As a result, the sisters scarcely differentiate; the role splitting apparent among other female siblings in Austen's novels is virtually nonexistent.

Austen does provide a happier model of sisterly behavior in Fanny's relationship with Susan. These sisters are companionable because they have not fought for parental attention or suitors during their separation. Moreover, both benefit when Fanny trains Susan. The latter acquires social niceties and manners, while Fanny begins to feel that she belongs and is useful. Like Anne Elliott, Fanny has practiced the art of self-effacement (as Leo Bersani states, "she almost *is not*"[31]), and she must assert herself in educating her sister.

The relationship between Fanny and Mary Crawford, a would-be sibling, provides another example of sisterly behavior. While the Bertrams' bond is completely negative, and the Prices' relationship is

educative, Mary at once helps and hinders Fanny. By encouraging the
heroine to accept Henry's proposal, Mary hopes to become her sister.
And when she plans to wed Edmund Bertram, who treats Fanny as a
"brother,"[32] Mary also stands to be Fanny's kin. Mary's gift of
Henry's chain (to bind Fanny?) reveals the duplicity of her motives as
well as of the suitor. Because she is a would-be sister rather than a
biological sibling, she is not completely enmeshed with Fanny, and
Fanny is free to reject her assistance. Moreover, Mary is an enabling
figure in spite of herself. She ultimately functions as the rival outside
the family who makes the heroine conscious of her love for a surrogate
brother.

R. F. Brissenden has remarked that Edmund's fraternal relationship
to Fanny "has distinctly incestuous overtones; and it is these . . . that
give the relationship between these two rather ordinary people its
underlying power."[33] As a brother, Edmund is appealing not only
because he replaces the distant William, but also because he offers an
apparently asexual, and hence nonthreatening, relationship. Edmund
emanates none of the uncontrolled sexuality that frightens Fanny in
Henry Crawford. Moreover, this match allows Fanny to stay at Mansfield Park, which has become her home.

With this essentially endogamous marriage, the conclusion of *Mansfield Park* offers a wider range of possibilities for sisters than the
closings of Austen's other novels. Fanny's marriage confirms her alliance with the Bertrams as well as her geographical and social distance
from the Prices. Like Kitty Bennet, Susan must be "improved" to be
imported to her sister's home, while William is permitted as an occasional visitor. The Bertram sisters are separated when Maria is banished. Perhaps the most intriguing aspect of the conclusion is the way
Austen treats unresolved conflicts in the older generation. Aunt Norris, whose constant meddling has served as an implied rebuke to Lady
Bertram, is finally displaced. It takes Maria's flight with Crawford—a
blow aimed in part at her own sister—to accomplish this displacement. Noxious and irritating siblings continue to be vanquished by
distance, but Austen admits the possibility once again of altering less
embarrassing sisters.

In *Emma,* Knightley, like Edmund Bertram, is presented in a
fraternal relationship to the heroine; he is Emma's brother-in-law.
Emma cannot recognize his love because she is preoccupied with her
relationship with her father. In fact, Emma acknowledges that one
reason for her eagerness to promote others' marriages is that she has
little desire to wed and leave her family. Thus, in this novel Austen
explores the dangers for the heroine who is too tightly enmeshed in the

family dynamic, a problem Gaskell later studies in *Wives and Daughters*.

Emma's closeness to her father, combined with role splitting, separates her from her sister Isabella, who has chosen to marry and start a family. The result is poor communication between the sisters throughout the novel. Emma may converse a great deal with her sister and father, but these discussions revolve around insignificant details pertaining to their health, drafts and the weather. This talk is scarcely more meaningful than the endless chatter of Miss Bates, which Emma mocks so harshly, or more expressive than Elizabeth Elliott's conversation. Crossed communications occur outside the family, too, most notably when Emma misinterprets the behavior of Jane Fairfax and Frank Churchill, but these errors are more comprehensible because they involve strangers. The weak communication at Hartfield is remarkable precisely because it occurs at home, where, as Gilbert and Gubar have noted:

> readiness to talk frequently masks reticence to communicate. . . . The civil falsehoods that keep society running make each character a riddle to the others, a polite puzzle.[34]

Not only are sisters "riddles" to each other, but each is unfamiliar with the part of herself that has been marked off as her sister's territory. For instance, Emma denies any interest in marrying, using "her social function as the concerned aunt to suppress her own unconscious love of Mr. Knightley and her jealousy at the very thought of his marrying anyone but herself."[35] Emma's insistence on seeing Knightley as nothing more than her brother-in-law prevents her from recognizing his suit, just as Fanny Price's determination to perceive Edmund Bertram as a surrogate brother allows her to ignore his sexuality. Emma's eventual decision to marry Knightley is therefore evidence of heightened self-awareness.

The foolish Isabella Knightley proves an intriguing alternative to Emma. While at first she appears merely a comic character, the contrast between her and Emma underlines the liabilities of too close an alignment with the father. As long as Emma gains power and status from her father's position in the village, she cannot leave home for long periods of time; she may enjoy being an aunt, but she will not be a parent. Isabella may not have the strength to stand up to her father on her own, but she uses her husband's whims and doctor's "orders" (which may or may not be fictive) to get her own way. Obsessions with physical comforts and health, inherited from Mr. Woodhouse, allow

Isabella to detach herself, instead of confining her in an incestuous bond. Characteristically feminine indirection is her primary mode of managing others; her manipulations are more effective than Emma's more direct and ambitious plans for others.

In *Emma*, Austen also takes up the problem of sisterhood. Like Anne Elliott, Fanny Price, and Elinor Dashwood, Emma lacks the companionship of peers. More importantly, without an effective model for friendship in her sisterly relationship, Emma does not know how to treat Jane Fairfax or Harriet Smith. She perceives them the way sisters so often see each other—as extensions of herself—and refuses to acknowledge their individuality or right to privacy. For example, Emma cannot separate her opinion of Jane from her estimation of herself. If she values Jane, she cannot approve of her own behavior:

> Why she did not like Jane Fairfax might be a difficult question to answer; Mr. Knightley had once told her it was because she saw in her the really accomplished young woman which she wanted to be thought herself; and though the accusation had been eagerly refuted at the time, there were moments of self-examination in which her conscience could not acquit her.[36]

The conclusion of *Emma* never truly resolves the problems of sisterhood or the heroine's excessive closeness to her father. Instead, Emma's marriage allows her to stay home with her father and to marry Knightley. One does not imagine her achieving her sister's independence from Mr. Woodhouse. The happiness at the end of the novel is forced; one also has difficulty picturing Knightley living contentedly in Mr. Woodhouse's household, and Emma remains separated from peers, Mrs. Weston being a social inferior. Emma is virtually a prisoner at Hartfield, satisfying two exigent men.

In the end, Austen's major novels suggest that the difficulties in achieving sisterhood are linked to unhappy sisterly relations. When marriage separates blood siblings, erasing their unhappiness, there is a possibility of sisterhood, but that possibility is tenuous at best. Although Elizabeth Bennet and Anne Elliott become friendly with Georgiana Darcy and Mrs. Croft, they lack a large circle of acquaintances, and Emma Woodhouse, too, remains isolated after her marriage. The world of heterosexual romance makes as little space for female friendship as it does for sisterly bonding.

Thus, sisters play a significant narrative and structural role in Austen's novels, but they ultimately form part of that darker underside, the reverse weave of the novel—what has to be suppressed, distanced or unfulfilled in a heroine for her to accept a traditional marriage and for the novelist to create a conventional ending. Like Psyche's sisters, the siblings in Austen's novels may in spite of themselves play an enabling role in the heroine's development, yet they are distanced with the completion of the marriage plot.

3

Elizabeth Gaskell
Embroidering the Pattern

Elizabeth Gaskell, like Jane Austen before her, traces the development of young women's identities in "emotionally significant pairs" of sisters.[1] But Gaskell does not envision the heroine's wedding as an inevitable conclusion to the sister plot. Instead of reinforcing the divisions between sisters with marriage, Gaskell offers alternative endings. She emphasizes the allure and danger of home: in *Cranford* and *The Life of Charlotte Brontë* she portrays young women who never marry or establish independent households, whereas in *Wives and Daughters* she focuses on a young woman whose marriage long seems unlikely. For Gaskell, friendships with other women, or sisterhoods, challenge heterosexual romances for priority in women's closest relationships outside the family.

Sisters are important in Gaskell's technical plan as well as in her thematic design. Role splitting takes on fixed patterns, and, as Arnold Rotner comments, the contrast between sisters "results in the novels being narrow in scope and well unified."[2] Although oppositions in Gaskell's novels may include other characters, Gaskell achieves the most drama and friction in the juxtaposition of two individuals who are as close as sisters. The greater the distance between characters, the less the tension; not as much is at stake in the relationship.

Gaskell's treatment of the sister bond is consistent with her experience, in contrast to Austen, whose intimacy with her sister is countered by often contentious relationships among fictive siblings. Gaskell's mother died when she was young, and she was raised by a widowed aunt in a household of women. Her father remarried, but Gaskell was never close to him or her new family. Her letters express a longing to be more intimate with her father, as well as disappointment in her stepmother and stepsisters, whom she saw only once in the twenty-five years following her father's death.

In raising her own children, Gaskell desired harmony, but not the peace created by identical interests. Her letters indicate that she wished her four daughters to avoid competition by developing different and complementary parts of themselves. Each girl's school was selected to meet her particular needs. Gaskell's hope for comradeship among her daughters may have sprung out of her own youthful isolation or out of a sense that solidarity, even dependence, among sisters was "right." Gaskell's remarks in a letter to her daughter Marianne imply that she took training manual warnings to heart:

> I could not bear my life if you and Meta did not love each other most dearly. . . . it is so dreary to see sisters grow old (as one sometimes does), not caring for each other, and forgetting all early home-ties.[3]

If Gaskell saw no evidence of closeness among sisters in the actuality of her past, she might project such intimacy into the future, not only for her daughters, but also for the heroines of her novels.

In discussing Gaskell's works, particularly *Cranford, Wives and Daughters*, and *The Life of Charlotte Brontë*, one must deal with two conflicting notions: an incomplete, repressive, yet powerful family and, in opposition, an impulse toward intimacy, which might be mythic, existing "as a reference, not as an actuality. . . ."[4] Critics who ignore this opposition limit their view of Gaskell's texts. David Cecil, for instance, comments that "bitterness and disillusion are as remote from Mrs. Gaskell's comprehension as violence. Every discord is resolvable to her. . . ."[5] One can hardly believe that Coral Lansbury is also describing Gaskell when she writes that

> she regarded it [the family] as a stifling and often blighting influence on children's lives. . . . Women's lives were stunted and children were forced to live with uncongenial siblings. . . . the happy families in the novels and stories have little in common with usual family patterns.[6]

The "happy families" referred to by Lansbury, exhibiting "little in common with usual family patterns" (what is usual?), may include metaphorical "sisters"—step-siblings, friends, and neighbors. Gaskell takes as a given a troubled or incomplete family and asks, how do we "make" family? What is family? Is it a fiction? What is a sister? What is the difference between a biological sister and a woman we choose to call "sister"? In her novels as well as in her biography of her friend Charlotte Brontë, she repeatedly addresses these issues, anticipating the difficulties apparent in twentieth-century criticism.

Gaskell sets the pattern for her treatment of sisters in two works preceding *Cranford—Mary Barton* and "Mr. Harrison's Confessions." Sisters are of marginal importance in the main plot of *Mary Barton*.

Unlike Austen's heroines, Mary has no sister. The heroine's mother dies in the third chapter of the novel, and the girl's aunt Esther is conspicuous primarily by her absence. Esther is the character excised from so much Victorian literature and discourse—the fallen woman, the prostitute. Yet Gaskell indicates that she is important nevertheless, making her the subject of the first line of dialogue.

Esther has just left home, and her disappearance causes her pregnant sister "overpowering and hysterical . . . grief."[7] Whereas Mrs. Barton is the sentimentalized Victorian mother, Esther is dangerously sexual. John Barton considers his wife's prettiness part of her maternal attraction, but he regards Esther's beauty as "a sad snare" (43). Power is the underlying issue; Esther's comeliness gives her self-confidence, and "there is no holding her in" (43). Mrs. Barton accepts her husband's severity, but her sister rebels and flees the hard, patriarchal "advice" (admonishments?) of John Barton (43). The sisters are complementary parts of one being. With the loss of Esther, female sexuality is virtually excluded from the novel, and Mrs. Barton cannot survive. Barton blames Esther's "giddiness, her lightness of conduct" (58), which is so often a euphemism for seductive female behavior, for his wife's death.

Young Mary's life is characterized by repression thereafter. She is unusually close to her remaining parent, restraining even her mourning "because it flashed across her mind that her violence of grief might disturb her father" (57). Nevertheless, "her mysterious aunt, Esther, had an unacknowledged influence over Mary" (63). The thought of the beautiful, distant Esther sets Mary apart from her peers and enables her to attract the patrician young Carson.

Every time Esther resurfaces, sexuality does, too. Once, she is taken for a drunk in a perverse equation of intoxication, sexuality, and loss of control in women. Next, she visits her niece to save Mary's lover, and, accidentally revealing the truth of John Barton's misconduct, she forces Mary to reconsider her closeness with her father. Thus, Esther points Mary in the direction of a fulfilling, adult sexuality (independent of John Barton), and away from her flirtation with Carson.

Having achieved her aim, Esther dies, and the heroine's acceptance of her sexuality is signaled by her marriage. While no such integration is apparent in Gaskell's later works, this novel is significant in illustrating Gaskell's division of sisters' personalities and in charting the effects of this split. Moreover, it offers an alternative ending to the sister story, one in which rejected qualities are assimilated by the heroine upon her marriage and the death of the sister/aunt.

In "Mr. Harrison's Confessions," a sketch for *Cranford*, a rural town is thrown into disarray by the arrival of an eligible young bachelor who titillates the local spinsters. As in Austen's novels, the hero of this story initially plays a brotherly role, which disguises and denies his sexuality. Mr. Harrison's housekeeper, the widowed Mrs. Rose, who has matrimonial designs on him, views him with "quite an older sister's interest. . . ."[8] The Misses Tompkinson are especially eager in their pursuit of Mr. Harrison, and their personalities prepare the reader for the differences between the Jenkyns sisters in *Cranford*. The younger, Miss Caroline, appears "very delicate and die-away"; she is "soft and sentimental," and easily "shocked at her sister's outré manners." In contrast, the "hard and masculine" Miss Tompkinson dominates her younger sister (415). The Tompkinsons are far less sympathetic than Matty and Deborah Jenkyns; moreover, perceived through the obtuse consciousness of the young doctor, these women remain stock figures, almost burlesques. The relationship between the siblings is never fully realized. They are a reminder of what the Misses Jenkyns might have been without the elaborate deceits of Cranford.

Unmarried and economically deprived, the Misses Jenkyns in *Cranford* are analogous to the ridiculous Miss Bates in *Emma*. However, although Gaskell's sisters occupy a marginal position within Victorian society, they are not objects of charity for the neighboring gentlemen. Their lives illustrate the intricate nexus of sex, power, class, and money in the novella: "The interest of *Cranford* comes from the tension between power and deprivation in its analysis of the etiquette of penury in the town of redundant women."[9]

Life in the Jenkyns home replicates the world of an Austen novel. Funds and affection are in limited supply, and the sisters have developed strategies to restrict competition for these commodities. By developing certain personal qualities in herself to the exclusion of others, each girl is able to attract her share of parental attention. Matty plays the part of the conventional woman. Her "mother's darling,"[10] she constantly fusses about her appearance, and she falls in love with Holbrook. In contrast, Deborah is renowned for her masculine headgear; she sports "a hybrid bonnet, half-helmet, half-jockey cap" (57). She adopts her father's righteousness and prefers the eighteenth-century rationality of Dr. Johnson's *Dictionary* to the humorous fictions of *Pickwick Papers*.

For a time, each sister is supplanted with her favorite parent by her brother Peter. However, Peter's failures soon restore Deborah to her place in her father's esteem (93). In contrast, Matty assumes a timid mien, considering herself inferior, not only because she is neither parent's favorite, but also because she has been identified with her mother, who is of secondary importance in the household. Instead of the occasional sharpness between sisters found in Austen novels (such as Elizabeth Elliott's scorn for Anne, or Elizabeth Bennet's mortification at Lydia's behavior), friction here is veiled, part of the euphemistic "elegant economy."

The girls' training produces repressed women. Matty is forced to relinquish her lover, Holbrook, because he is of an inferior social rank. Unlike Emma Woodhouse, Deborah is never able to detach herself sufficiently from her father's influence to marry. Matty hints at the irony and futility of the sacrifice, pointing out that Deborah prides herself on rejecting nonexistent proposals. Nevertheless, being the model daughter gives Deborah stature in the parish:

> She was such a daughter to my father, as I think there never was before, or since. His eyes failed him, and she read book after book, and wrote, and copied, and was always at his service in any parish business. (102)

In this passage, Gaskell refers to the sacrifices of Milton's daughter in his blindness, neatly blending the allusion with an intimation of the unusually close (and almost incestuous) nature of the father-daughter bond. If Elizabeth Bennet is admitted to the sanctum of her father's study and Emma Woodhouse caters to her father's every whim, Deborah Jenkyns goes one step further. Her father's amanuensis, she is literally his extension, a part of him.

What is repressed and banished, as in *Mary Barton*, is adult sexuality; it is vanquished and disposed of in Peter's Oedipal struggle with his father. Rather than confront the awesome interdiction of Reverend Jenkyns, Peter prefers to "plague" Deborah, his father's weaker extension. Peter's assault, although indirect, reaches its target. By masquerading as Deborah cradling a baby, he affronts his sister's honor and challenges his father's power, implying to the townsfolk that someone has replaced Reverend Jenkyns in his favorite's affections, essentially emasculating the reverend. Indeed, the transfer of power is apparent when Peter comes in after his masquerade, "looking like a man, not like a boy" (102). But Peter does not succeed completely, for his father flogs him, reestablishing his physical authority, and, like Esther in *Mary Barton*, Peter is forced to flee. As long as he is under his father's roof, he is under his father's dominance and cannot assert mature sexuality without reprisal. His departure corresponds to the banishment of sexuality from the family; the possibility of fulfillment for his sisters goes with him. No one remains to challenge the reverend.

Soon afterward, Mrs. Jenkyns dies, and her death, like that of Mary Barton's mother, is another sign of the exclusion of sexuality from the story. Deborah stays with the rector, with Matty as her companion. Yet Deborah, try as she may to assist her father with parish duties, can never replace Mrs. Jenkyns (102). In assisting her father, she has chosen the realm of the study rather than the kitchen. If she were to replace her mother, she would have to relinquish some of her privileges. In part, too, she is unable to take her mother's place because she has not developed her sexuality. She cannot give the rector children, which would be visible proof to the world of his continuing power and, in a way, of his immortality.

Instead, evidence of the girls' repression abounds in the novel, from their discomfort with servants having "followers" (as if men were mere appendages), to their retreat to their bedrooms when indulging in the suggestive act of sucking oranges. The completeness of their ignorance is most apparent when Matty is genuinely unaware of Martha's advanced pregnancy.

Initially, Matty is stunted by this repression and by her sister's dominance. Miss Jenkyns, as Patsy Stoneman has noted, "has assimilated the conditions of her own subordination."[11] She criticizes Major Brown for enjoying Dickens and tyrannizes her younger sister. The patriarchal authority Deborah assumes extends to censoring her sister's thoughts:

> Miss Matilda Jenkyns (who did not mind being called Miss Matty, when Miss Jenkyns was not by) wrote nice, kind rambling letters; now and then venturing into an opinion of her own; but suddenly pulling herself up, and either begging me not to name what she had said, as Deborah thought differently, and *she* knew; or else putting in a . . . recantation of every opinion she had given in the letter. (51)

Miss Jenkyns, having taken "the Hebrew prophetess for a model in character" (51), exerts such power that, even after her death, her younger sister constantly defers to what she imagines to be her wishes. Although Deborah's unwise investment leads to Matty's ruin, Matty never voices criticism or anger, so reluctant is she to betray Deborah's principles. The younger Miss Jenkyns has come to depend on Deborah's standards; replacing her father's authoritative commands (rather than maternal affection), they provide a secure set of guidelines for her conduct, ordering her life and shaping her story.

Martin Dodsworth's assertion that "Miss Matty is made a scapegoat for the sins of her sister"[12] is partly true then. But in many ways the death of Miss Jenkyns allows Matty to find subtle ways of altering the order at Cranford. When Holbrook reappears, only to die shortly afterward, Matty reveals the seriousness of her emotions by wearing widow's caps. Matty also gives Martha permission to see young men, allowing her servant what her sister forbade her.

Although Matty longs for a turban to wear to Signor Bruoni's conjuring performance and grows more assertive after her sister's death, she never assumes Deborah's masculine headgear or domineering tone. With the loss of her income, Matty is forced for "the first time in her life . . . to choose anything of consequence for herself . . ." (173). Even though she worries about how her refined sister might have judged her, Matty opens a business: "I don't think, if Deborah knows where she is, she'll care so very much if I'm not genteel . . ." (196).

Without Deborah, Miss Matty must acknowledge money and sex, the two greatest subjects of repression in her life. The polite fictions of the town allow her to do so evasively; she affects not to notice much about Martha's growing attachment to Jem, and she gives away so many of her candies that it is scarcely as if she is in business at all. She succeeds not by adopting masculine traits, like her sister, but by subverting traditional femininity. Although Deborah is not alive to condemn her sister's commercial venture, such critics as Martin Dodsworth are troubled by Matty's shopkeeping. Preferring to categorize *Cranford* as "a novel of escape," Dodsworth finds "psychological accuracy . . . strangely out of place in a genre noted for evasion. . . ."[13] Yet in fact the "psychological accuracy" is entirely appropriate. For Gaskell, the "evasion" of *Cranford* is its "psychological accuracy"; spinster ladies like Miss Matty, to retain their position and respect, have to work by devious means, clothing their cows in flannel waistcoats and leaving signs of a masculine presence in their homes to deter burglars. In *Communities of Women*, Nina Auerbach notes that such little stratagems give the Amazons of Cranford what power they have: "Part of its [the female community's] artillery is the power of deceit."[14]

The unmarried women in the community are remarkable for their similarity to Matty, while her relationship with her sister is defined by difference. Role splitting characterizes the bond of blood sisters, but mutual affinities define relations among friends, or sisters by choice. As a result, fictive kin relationships are altogether less tense than those among blood relatives. In *Cranford*, for instance, Matty's friends share her nocturnal terrors, her excitement about fashion, and her bewilderment over finances. The sisterhood assists her when she has lost her money as a result of her sister's unwise investment. And, even as the women enable her to perpetuate the myth of her gentility, they are her audience. For them, she survives the dark chill of trimmed candles lit alternately; for them, she engages in curious maneuvers to prevent the sun from fading her carpet. Matty's relationship with her sister is controlled by her father even after his death, but the sisterhood's main characteristic is its subversiveness. Even as it enables Matty to undermine patriarchal conventions, it pretends to support them.

The end of the story is evasive, too. A man comes to the rescue, but he is no Prince Charming, no suitor in the guise of a brother, like two heroes of Austen's novels, Knightley and Bertram. Gaskell offers only Peter Jenkyns, Matty's biological brother. Moreover, Peter does not bring back sexuality. He has been emasculated; like an old umbrella, Peter is no more than a "stick" in "petticoats" (40), and "there is no need for him to dress in women's clothes for he shares the very spirit of Cranford."[15] Peter joins the community, participating in the endless rounds of tea, the quiet gambling over cards (the only permissible risk in Cranford), the gossip and storytelling, at which he becomes proficient.

In all the excitement and bounty of Peter's return, an important secret is ignored: "Gaskell has Peter 'save' Matty from an evidently successful enterprise. . . ."[16] As Peter assumes Deborah's position as the eldest, his sister becomes "my little Matty" (208) again. Recent events are erased, and Matty's newfound independence is forgotten. Her business is closed, and, significantly, the spirit of Deborah rises from the grave in one last gesture, "the handsomest bound and best edition of Dr. Johnson's works" is presented to the narrator as a gift from both sisters (211). The text of the father thus resurfaces to impose rigid definitions on words and to discourage the laxity that allowed feminine evasiveness to flourish.

Elizabeth Gaskell does insert an alternative sister story in the work when she traces the fortunes of Jessie Brown. Jessie's courtship is completed, but Gaskell implies that marriage is not necessarily a happier solution. Both Jessie's father and her sister die before she can marry. Once she is Mrs. Gordon, Jessie is not allowed to continue in the female economy of Cranford; she may return only as a visitor. In a later short story, "The Cage at Cranford," she introduces the village to a mysterious and controversial item. The cagelike crinoline she sends represents an outsider's view of the oppressive existence of single women in the village.

Although Matty experiences a temporary and limited independence after Deborah dies, the death of a sister does not permit Matty to leave Cranford's cage. Nor does it allow her to achieve a fully integrated, mature personality of her own; as in the stories of Jessie Brown and Psyche, sisters' deaths confirm the heroine's submission to male authority. Moreover, the division between sisters is not reinforced by status or geography following marriage as in Austen's novels, for the heroine never leaves home. Instead, Matty's primary relationships outside the family are with a sisterhood of other spinsters, who join her in the feminine game of evasion, the pretenses to wealth and comfort in the midst of deprivation and powerlessness. Similar deceits may exist in the world outside Cranford, but here, the heroine is more fully insulated by her circle of acquaintances. By her hearth, Matty is surrounded by the happy faces of her brother as well as the women who supported her in her misfortunes. And they, once again, help her to create a fiction. With them, it is as if Matty's life had never changed. The novel ends in the permanent childhood of romance, in a world where delicate lace can be retrieved from the belly of a cat.

In this realm of romance, the tensions of relations among blood sisters seem supplanted by an idyllic vision of sisterhood. The paternal dominance of the family home appears to give way to a female community defined and sustained by its efforts to undermine male power. Yet, although the sister story generated by patriarchal authority is challenged, it is not replaced by the vision of female solidarity, which is itself a fiction. The rosy cheerfulness of the final scenes of *Cranford* emphasizes that the vision is just that, a vision. Because the sisterhood is defined by its subversiveness, it remains controlled and threatened by male assumptions and expectations. In the end, Gaskell's female community in *Cranford* prepares for the complex questions concerning fiction, sisterhood, and idealism raised by her own *Life of Charlotte Brontë* as well as by recent works of feminist criticism.

Nina Auerbach's discussion of *Cranford* in *Communities of Women*, which has been cited above, includes many astute observations. Yet Auerbach's analysis is also an excellent example of the way feminist critics have treated Gaskell's work as an unambiguous celebration of sisterhood. Auerbach scarcely refers to Deborah Jenkyns; perceiving her entirely as the rector's alter ego, Auerbach equates Deborah's death with the demise of patriarchal authority in Cranford.[17] As she emphasizes Matty's fragile independence, Auerbach glorifies the sisterhood of spinsters and neglects to indicate the extent to which Matty's behavior continues to be affected by her sister's opinions. Thus, for Auerbach, the sister plot is replaced by a plot that promotes sisterhood.

The consequences of rejecting one plot in favor of another are perhaps most apparent in Auerbach's contradictory statements about the realism of *Cranford*. While both the male and female worlds of *Cranford* are fictive, Auerbach seems determined to give primacy to the collective creation of a female community. She initially refers to the novella as a "rural idyll," but then comments on the town's "idyllic *veneer*" (emphasis added), as if the town only appears to be part of a fantasy. Similarly, she begins by setting the town in contrast to the "harsh industrial world" and by praising its "cohesion against the world," as if it were outside reality. These comments are followed by the paradoxical claim that the community "appropriates the reality it excludes," and ultimately by assertions that the sisterhood has co-opted reality, "defeat[ing] the warrior world that proclaims itself the real one."[18] In this process, Auerbach "proclaims" her vision of sisterhood "the real one," as opposed to the patriarchal tradition of male power that dominates sisterly relationships.

In such criticism, Gaskell's intricate portrait of the female community created in reaction to the patriarchy and continually threatened by it is replaced by a vision that emphasizes only the strengths of sisterhood. However, in her last novel, *Wives and Daughters*, Gaskell once again reveals how relations among women are defined by patriarchal authority, and she cautions against a facile glorification of sisterhood.

The fragile happiness of the spinsters at the end of *Cranford* is moved away from center stage in *Wives and Daughters*, where the Misses Browning are not major characters. *Wives and Daughters* is a more traditional Victorian novel than *Cranford*. It has a marriage plot involving two charming young heroines and assorted suitors, one of whom is threatening and villainous even as he is revoltingly mediocre. While *Cranford* refers ironically to the archetypal Amazons, *Wives and Daughters* alludes most directly to "Cinderella"; like the latter, *Wives and Daughters* may be considered a sister story, because it, too, involves step-siblings whose lives recapitulate the knotty problems of identity and independence found among blood kin.

In *Wives and Daughters*, as in "Cinderella," the heroine's intimacy with her father precedes her ties with her step-family. Molly is the quintessential "daddy's girl," bound in a relationship that ultimately determines the nature of her sisterly bond. Therefore, although this relationship may appear peripheral to our discussion, it must be treated in depth.

Initially, Molly Gibson leads an idyllic existence, adored by the household servants and protected by her widowed father. Molly's desire that she and her father should "never lose each other,"[19] although childish prattle, has a sinister aspect. After she is accidentally left behind at the home of the local gentry, Molly wishes to be "chained" to the doctor (58), in a bond that would be a physical manifestation of her emotional dependence. Mr. Gibson enjoys considerably more power in the relationship than Molly; as she herself remarks, he may know that she wants him, but he need not come (58). And Mr. Gibson, instead of reassuring his daughter, teases her. Mr.

Gibson's joking is only superficially affectionate paternal banter; it masks his unwillingness to respond adequately to the emotional content of his daughter's appeals:

> But even to her, in their most private moments, he did not give way to much expression of his feelings; his most caressing appellation for her was 'Goosey', and he took a pleasure in bewildering her infant mind with his badinage. He had rather a contempt for demonstrative people, arising from his medical insight into the consequences to health of uncontrolled feeling. (63)

Under a veneer of affection, Mr. Gibson is the stereotypical father of Victorian novels, domineering, manipulative, afraid of feminine emotion, and of what is so often referred to as "uncontrolled"—sexuality. He is another version of the fathers in Austen's novels as well as of those in Gaskell's *Cranford* and *Mary Barton*. In deflecting Molly's entreaties with humor, he protects himself, even as he offers her just enough affection to keep her longing for more.

The repressive nature of Mr. Gibson's character is further apparent in his attitude toward his daughter's education. He hires a governess, Miss Eyre (after the heroine of Charlotte Brontë's novel?), not to train Molly to be a young woman, but "to keep her a child . . ." (65). He concedes to "the prejudices of society" (65) in allowing Molly to learn reading and writing. But his daughter, a true descendant of Eve, thirsts for knowledge: "It was only by fighting and struggling hard, that bit by bit Molly persuaded her father to let her have French and drawing lessons" (65). The biblical parallel is strengthened by a subtle allusion: "She read every book that came in her way, almost with as much delight as if it had been forbidden" (65). Intellectual pursuits hold for Molly all the allure of forbidden fruit; despite her father's efforts, she is avid for knowledge.

The incestuous nature of Molly's relationship with her father, which is a variant of the alliances in *Emma, Pride and Prejudice,* and *Cranford*, is underscored when she experiences a kind of fall. In fact, Molly's story from this point on provides an alternative to Deborah Jenkyns's continued closeness with her father. When Mr. Gibson intercepts a note from one of his apprentices to Molly, he is quick to interdict this text, too. Expelled from the "Eden of childhood,"[20] Molly is sent to stay with family friends, the Hamleys. A further result of Molly's "fall" is the loss of her exclusive relationship with her father, as Mr. Gibson seeks a second wife to protect Molly at home. In his proposal, "mother" precedes "wife," making Gibson's intentions perfectly clear (140).

Although Angus Easson is correct in not wishing to "press the analogy too far," Molly does perceive Mrs. Gibson as a "wicked stepmother."[21] She misreads her father's motives, believing that Mrs. Kirkpatrick, who has been sought to keep her at home, is the cause of her banishment. As Coral Lansbury asserts, "Molly's reaction to the news of her father's forthcoming marriage is less that of a daughter than a lover or wife."[22] But Mr. Gibson's training serves him well, and Molly suppresses her jealousy:

> She was afraid of saying anything, lest the passion of anger, dislike, indignation—whatever it was that was boiling up inside her breast—should find vent in cries and screams, or worse, in raging words that could never be forgotten. It was as if the piece of solid ground on which she stood had broken from the shore, and she was drifting out to the infinite sea alone. (145)

Molly's silence is convenient for Mr. Gibson, who has "half-guessed" her anguish; it allows him to persist in the illusion that he is doing what is best for her and to retain his power over her. Mr. Gibson may not be as intimidating as the Reverend Jenkyns, but his power is equally effective.

Molly is a better pupil than her father could imagine, and, ultimately, "masculine silence promotes not only dutiful self-suppression but deviousness and evasion in women. . . ."[23] She becomes manipulative, the covert nature of her stratagems indicated by the passive voice, which obscures Molly's role in household arrangements: " 'Somehow' it was managed. 'Somehow' all Molly's wishes came to pass . . ." (488). Molly succeeds in persuading the physician to take her on his rounds while her stepmother is out of town, during which time father and daughter are "quite like bride and bridegroom . . ." (488), sharing cozy meals at home and being entertained by the townspeople. Evidently, had Mr. Gibson not remarried, he would have had his dearest wish, perpetual and uninterrupted "happy intercourse" (488) with his daughter, and Molly's life would have duplicated the existence of Deborah Jenkyns. It is no wonder, then, that Hyacinth Clare Kirkpatrick feels she must compete with her stepdaughter, just as she earlier vied with her daughter Cynthia for Preston's attentions.

Molly's quasi-incestuous bond with her father determines not only the hostile nature of her relationship with her stepmother but also the quality of her interactions with her new sister. Critics have compared Molly's rivalry with Cynthia for the love of Roger Hamley to Fanny Price's competition with Mary Crawford in *Mansfield Park*.[24] However, while Austen emphasizes the lack of sisterly relations among Fanny, the Bertram girls, and Mary Crawford, Gaskell wishes her characters to be considered siblings and notes in a letter to her publisher that "these two girls—contrasting characters,—not sisters but living as sisters in the same house are unconscious rivals for the love of a young man. . . ."[25] Although Cynthia and Molly are not raised together, the girls resemble biological siblings because they have no opportunity to select each other and are bound for life by (or because of) their parents' marriage. Furthermore, like blood sisters, they must compete for resources, including parental attention and the love of eligible suitors. This rivalry is "unconscious"; like the blood sisters in Austen's novels, these girls go to tremendous lengths to avoid and deny their competition.

Initially, Gaskell performs the feat of gradually transforming two strangers into sisters. Molly begins by stating that sharing her home with Cynthia "will almost be like having a sister" (192). Later, although Molly has difficulty calling Clare "mamma" (207), she has no difficulty in accepting Cynthia, because the latter is not a rival for the man who matters most to Molly, her father. Besides,

> Cynthia had so captivated Molly, that she wanted to devote herself to the new-comer's service. Ever since she had heard of the probability of her having a sister—(she called her a sister, but whether it was a Scotch sister, or a sister à la mode de Bretagne, would have puzzled more people)—Molly had allowed her fancy to dwell much on the idea of Cynthia's coming. . . . (254)

Cynthia's initial attraction is akin to a seduction: "Molly fell in love with her, so to speak, on the instant" (253). Eventually, Cynthia's affection and growing intimacy replace continual, uninterrupted closeness with Mr. Gibson in Molly's life. The daughter thus compensates in part for the havoc her mother creates, and with her chatty stepsister, Molly finds an outlet for the emotions she has had to repress in her father's presence.

From the start, Gaskell indicates that the girls' closeness is not a result of similarity but of "contrasting characters" developed through their separate upbringings. While Molly continues to dress childishly, Cynthia "look[s] quite a woman" (252). Molly is tousled, often shabby and in need of new garments, but Cynthia's clothes are always neat and elegant (in this, if nothing else, she is her mother's daughter). Finally, Molly is innocent in the ways of men, whereas Cynthia is adept in the arts of flirtation and seduction and has contracted a clandestine engagement. Molly has been raised under her father's thumb; Cynthia has been trained among women.

Gaskell's use of contrasting personalities at this point in the novel is not limited to sisters. Gaskell provides a pair of brothers, Roger and Osborne Hamley, but they only underline the differences between brothers' and sisters' relationships. Although Osborne and Roger must share limited funds, and Roger makes sacrifices to pay Osborne's debts, Gaskell restricts their competition in other areas. Osborne marries a French woman, and he is thus removed from the Hollingsford marriage market. Moreover, the loss of funds to pay Osborne's debts does not truly hinder Roger's prospects; instead, he succeeds as a naturalist and comes to represent the man of the future. Osborne, the older son and his parents' promise, withers and dies in a feminine decline. For brothers then, Gaskell finds ways out of the family; only the sibling who does not grasp the chance to escape suffers the feminine ending.

In contrast, the girls' carefully demarcated roles do not prevent competition for lovers. Indeed, the situation in this novel resembles that in several of Austen's works. With Osborne's marriage and his removal as an eligible partner for one of the girls, both find themselves attracted to Roger, and relationships in the novel become fluid. Prior to this point, Molly has repeatedly been compared to Roger's dead sister, Fanny, and she has stood in a fraternal relationship to him (284). He has shown her "brotherly kindness" (280), and, indeed, were he to marry Cynthia, he would be a kind of brother to Molly. Like Edmund Bertram with Fanny Price, Roger has provided Molly with the learning after which she thirsts in opposition to her father's wishes. He has also consoled her about her father's remarriage. His presence as a surrogate male relative helps her to overcome her grief.

Like Fanny Price in *Mansfield Park*, Molly finds herself the confidante of the man she loves in his courtship of another. Trained to repress negative emotions, Molly never acknowledges the competition, but Gaskell signals the situation by entitling the chapter in which it appears "Rivalry." The contention is especially hurtful to Molly because Cynthia and Roger's love excludes her; she is no longer first with either of the individuals who have come closest to replacing her father in her heart.

Once the rivalry arises, Molly resents being called Cynthia's sister. She affects "indifference" to the matter, as if she had never enjoyed the appellation, and attempts to distance herself from Cynthia:

Now Molly's love for Cynthia was fast and unwavering, but if anything tried it, it was the habit Roger had fallen into of always calling Cynthia Molly's sister in speaking of the latter. From any one else it would have been a matter of indifference to her, and hardly to be noticed; it vexed both her ear and heart when Roger used the expression. . . . (355)

The pain in the passage reveals that Molly's love for Cynthia is anything but "fast and unwavering." Molly's disingenuousness about being called Cynthia's sister reveals divided loyalties. As a "good" sister, Molly believes she should not envy Cynthia's fortune; as a "good" friend, she should be happy that Roger is in love. But she has feelings she does not acknowledge for Roger. As the girls' undeclared rivalry grows, their differences are accentuated, too:

> The two girls seemed to have parted company in cheerfulness. Molly was always gentle, but very grave and silent. Cynthia, on the contrary, was merry, full of pretty mockeries, and hardly ever silent. (388)

Significantly, Mrs. Gaskell next refers to Cynthia as Molly's "friend" (389), not her sister. The division represents a rupture in identity. In the same paragraph, Molly perceives Cynthia's "constant brilliancy" as "the glitter of pieces of a broken mirror, which confuses and bewilders" (389). Molly is looking at the parts of what she could have been, longing for wholeness. She is "confused" because she desires (to be) Cynthia, the other, sexual half of self, and to be loved by Roger. Yet, like Mary Barton and the Jenkyns siblings, she remains imprisoned in her father's standards, so that she feels she has no right to such happiness. She persists instead in blaming herself for being upset at the "natural" attraction between Roger and Cynthia (389).

Molly's sense of guilt at not being "good" results in her trying even harder. Because the standard of "goodness" she has inherited from her father consists above all of restraint, Molly strives to appear controlled and loyal, defending Roger and Cynthia: "What seemed neither to hurt Roger nor annoy Cynthia made Molly's blood boil . . ." (356). Molly replaces guilt with protective anger because she considers the former an unfeminine emotion. No wonder Roger prefers Cynthia, she seems to think.

As Molly keeps trying to please, she must continue to repress her genuine sorrow. As Patricia Spacks comments, "She becomes good, people are always telling her how good she is. But she is not happy: and finally she falls into the familiar Victorian decline. . . ."[26] The self-destructive nature of the behavior is apparent in the text: "She would have been willing to cut off her right hand, if need were, to forward his [Roger's] attachment to Cynthia; and the self sacrifice would have added a strange zest to a happy crisis" (390). Molly's "strange zest" at the possibility of "sacrifice" echoes Elizabeth Bennet's combined pleasure and pain regarding Lydia's behavior. As always, sisters' emotions are mixed. If Molly is not to benefit from having the man of her choice, she will gain satisfaction from her martyrdom for the sake of her worldly stepsister.

Ultimately, Molly's sacrifices are maturing; as a result of her relationships with women, she is able to achieve the adulthood her father has denied her. Mrs. Hamley's death and Mrs. Gibson's failure to behave in a motherly fashion create a gap that Molly begins to fill by nurturing others. She courageously retrieves Cynthia's letters from Preston (though no one rescued Mr. Coxe's letter for her); thus, Cynthia "regresses, as it were, to a child; while Molly . . . enacts a mother's role. . . ."[27] In addition, Molly's "maternal influence" is apparent in the Hamley household, where she provides comfort and solace after the death of Mrs. Hamley.[28]

Molly's transformed self is not entirely maternal. Patsy Stoneman characterizes the end of the novel as a revision of the Cinderella myth that emphasizes sisterhood rather than motherhood: "The positive quality derives from female friendship. There is wry satisfaction in Cynthia/Cinderella being rescued not by but from a Prince Charming, and by a Molly. . . ."[29] In sisterhood, it seems, one can play the saving role of the fairy godmother (as Matty Jenkyns's friends pitch in to help her in her financial distress).

This redefinition of Molly's role is crucial in the conclusion of the novel. *Wives and Daughters* again echoes *Mansfield Park*, for when Cynthia rejects Roger, Molly remains to comfort him. Mr. Gibson finds himself in competition with another man for his daughter's affections: "'Lover *versus* father!' thought he, half sadly. 'Lover wins'" (701). Mrs. Gaskell never completed the novel, so we cannot know how Mr. Gibson resolves his trouble. Perhaps like Austen's Mr. Bennet he remains a frequent visitor in his daughter's home, seeing it as a haven from his wife's importunities. Perhaps, too, he finally realizes that, if he retains possession of his daughter, he loses a primary source of his power over her, his ability to dispose of her at will in the marriage market. Jane Gallop points out the danger of incest when women are valued as commodities: "If the father were to desire his daughter he could no longer exchange her, no longer possess her in the economy by which true, masterful possession is the right to exchange."[30] In the very act of giving his daughter's hand in marriage, then, Dr. Gibson asserts his power. One cannot cede authority one does not possess.

Like the concluding marriages in Austen's novels, this one is not entirely satisfying. Gaskell's heroine marries a man who has been tarnished by his love for a flighty young girl. He is a man of science, like Molly's father, and not a man of emotion. In *The Adolescent Idea*, Patricia Spacks questions the dynamics of the ending:

> Does Molly's getting the man she wants sufficiently compensate for what she has endured? At a deeper level, the happy-ending match seems virtually irrelevant. . . . The more profound story . . . shows Molly turning inward rather than outward, . . . developing psychological rather than sexual power: the power of limited needs.[31]

In focusing upon Molly's psychological rather than sexual influence, Spacks implies that Molly is never a fully integrated character. Sexuality remains split off in Cynthia, who, like Mary Crawford, is sent to London, that center of masculine power and iniquity. As in an Austen novel, competition is excised, made unnecessary by geographical distance. But here, distance takes on a different dimension. The young women are no longer perceived (and no longer perceive themselves) as sisters; rather, they are friends, part of a sisterhood. They no longer need to be close but have chosen to be so. Even the novel's title erases the crucial sororal relationship.

At the end of *Wives and Daughters*, Gaskell creates a paradoxical situation in which sisters must deny their relationship, their very familiarity, in order to be close, to achieve a sisterhood. As in *Cranford*, they find greater support in a sisterhood than in a blood relationship created by paternal (and patriarchal) power. And, as in *Cranford*, their sisterhood is a creation. In fact, in the later novel, Gaskell emphasizes the idea that all relationships among women are metaphors; the girls' decision to engage in sisterhood merely revises their initial choice to be like blood sisters.

In *The Life of Charlotte Brontë*, on the other hand, Gaskell attempts what appears to be the reverse—turning a friend into a sister. However, to succeed in this task, Gaskell must separate Brontë from her blood siblings; thus for Brontë, the "heroine" of the story, the biography repeats the plot of *Cranford* and *Wives and Daughters*, as she is moved from closeness with her sisters into a sisterhood with Gaskell.

In discussing this work and Gaskell's motivation in writing it, one must consider the nature of the biographical and critical impulse in women writers. What is the satisfaction women gain from writing about other women authors? Is it the same fulfillment anyone—male or female—might gain from writing a life?

The claim that any biography is truthful is problematic, if not spurious; in the case of Gaskell's biography of Brontë, the issue is especially complex, and it is relevant to the themes of sisters and sisterhood. Indeed, from the beginning of Gaskell's text it is clear that narrative demands supersede fact. Some of Gaskell's material comes from the hearsay of a dismissed servant. She suppresses controversial information after acknowledging requests from Brontë's family, questioning her own instincts, and receiving threats of litigation. Arthur

Pollard has commented that in the end the work so ennobles its subject that "*The Life* was an intentional piece of hagiography."[32] But Gaskell's evasions and emphases do not merely glorify Charlotte Brontë. They also shed light on Gaskell's needs and ambivalences. The act of writing the biography obviously raised questions about closeness and family for Gaskell herself; significantly, she visited her stepmother and stepsister for the first time in twenty-five years while she was writing the biography.[33]

Most of all, the initial situation of *The Life* resembles that in one of Gaskell's novels: three young sisters in a small town struggle under the tyranny of a widowed father. Gaskell's care in depicting the setting and in capturing its atmosphere in the opening chapters reveals everywhere a shaping hand. She makes no attempt to be objective when she describes the moors as

> grand, from the ideas of solitude and loneliness which they suggest, or oppressive from the feeling which they give of being pent-up by some monotonous and illimitable barrier, according to the mood of mind in which the spectator might be.[34]

Both moods, "grandeur" and "oppression," prepare for the claustrophobic aura of the parsonage.

The fictive quality of the memoir is heightened when the sisters are introduced not as living persons but as completed texts, their lives neatly summarized on stone tablets in the church. The story's conclusion is predetermined and available, as in a work of fiction (where one can surreptitiously peek at the closing) rather than in life. Finally, Gaskell's tactic of quoting letters extensively as testimony contributes to the similarity between *The Life* and a novel, for, ironically, the use of the epistolary form with an accompanying claim to veracity is one of the oldest novelistic techniques extant. Referring to the arguments swirling around the first edition of *The Life of Charlotte Brontë*, Alan Shelston correctly notes that "Mrs. Gaskell had ideal material for a novel, but she seems to have forgotten that it was not a novel she was writing."[35]

Patrick Brontë, as presented in the early chapters of the book, is indeed the typical patriarch of Gaskell's novels.[36] He is as irascible as John Barton and as stern as the rector of Cranford. Mr. Brontë consistently appears in this awesome guise in the memoir, from the time he shreds his wife's bright green dress (89) until he objects to Charlotte's late marriage as if she were a "child to be guided and ruled" (508).

Like Molly Gibson, the Brontë girls are shaped by paternal authority. They quickly learn from their father to suppress their "wild strong hearts" and "powerful minds" (are these euphemisms for sexuality and intellectual creativity?), burying them "under an enforced propriety and rigidity of demeanour and expression, just as their faces had been concealed by their father, under his stiff unchanging mask" (108). Gaskell also records traces of Patrick Brontë's domination in the juvenilia: "There is hardly one of her prose-writings at this time in which . . . their 'august father' does not appear as a sort of Jupiter Tonans or Deus ex Machinâ" (120).

Patrick Brontë's commanding sternness, together with the remote situation of the Haworth parsonage, limits the girls' ability to marry or leave home, and it constitutes a similarity to the situation in *Cranford*. The sisters lack the skills to mingle in social settings, and at least one of them has to remain at the parsonage to nurse a succession of invalids: an aunt, Patrick Brontë, their brother Branwell, an aging servant, or one of themselves. The deaths of the two eldest Brontë sisters at school make travel and distance appear even more dangerous, as "Charlotte Brontë learned to associate any departure from Haworth with suffering and death."[37]

More than in *Cranford* and *Wives and Daughters*, Gaskell feels compelled to make the sibling relationship in *The Life* fit the Victorian model of feminine harmony. Her portrait of the sisters' affectionate interdependence has laid the groundwork for an idealization of their bond. However, these glorified myths ignore the fact that Gaskell's portrait relies on differences between the sisters. She stresses the deleterious effects of paternal oppression and emotional deprivation as well as the sisters' development of individual roles to avoid competition.

Critics, who may be seeking "sisters" themselves, commonly attempt to fuse the sisters. For instance, in *Communities of Women*, Nina Auerbach stresses the sisters' "unity." Her view is consistent with her glorification of the community of women in *Cranford*: "To her [Elizabeth Gaskell], the sisters' dream of founding a school for girls is . . . a means of consecrating their unity by living together." Moreover, Auerbach merges the Brontës' pseudonymous personas: "In their essence, Currer, Ellis, and Acton Bell *were* one person to Elizabeth Gaskell, and the lash that drives them apart is treated with all the outrage of a broken covenant."[38]

In fact, Gaskell goes to great lengths to separate Charlotte from her sisters (the book is entitled *The Life of Charlotte Brontë*, after all, and not *The Life of the Brontë Sisters*). The vision of harmony among the siblings ultimately appears more as a longing than as an actuality. In numerous passages, Gaskell draws distinctions among the girls' personalities as carefully as Austen delineates the characters of the Bennets. She cites the comparisons in Ellen Nussey's introduction to Charlotte's siblings at length:

> Emily was a tall, long-armed girl, more fully grown than her elder sister; extremely reserved in manner. . . . Anne, like her eldest sister, was shy; Emily was reserved. (147)

Mrs. Gaskell makes equally fine distinctions when describing Branwell's portrait of his sisters, but here, as in her novels, she creates an opposition by comparing Emily and Anne to "twins" (178),[39] and setting the younger girls apart from Charlotte. For Gaskell, a "pillar," which might not appear so "great" to others, "divides" the portrait:

> On the side of the column which was lighted by the sun, stood Charlotte, in the womanly dress of that day of jigot [sic] sleeves and large collars. On the deeply shadowed side, was Emily, with Anne's gentle face resting on her shoulder. Emily's countenance struck me as full of power; Charlotte's of solicitude; Anne's of tenderness. (155)

Gaskell cannot resist imagining that the light is a manifestation of Charlotte's special, happier fate: "I had some fond superstitious hope that the column divided their fates from hers, who stood apart in the canvas, as in life she survived. I liked to see that the bright side of the pillar was toward her—that the light in the picture fell on her . . ." (155). Thus, Gaskell picks out her own "sister" in the portrait.

Much as differences are significant to Gaskell, she does not portray all three of the sisters equally. The imperative to focus on an "emotionally significant pair" and to use their contrasts to heighten her depiction of character is apparent here, as it is in Austen's novels. As the biography progresses, Mrs. Gaskell concentrates especially on the differences between Emily and Charlotte, allowing Anne to fade away. She attempts to turn Charlotte into a calm, gentle Victorian heroine, a Molly Gibson or a Mary Barton. It is no wonder then that, in *Woman and the Demon*, Nina Auerbach reads Gaskell's biography as a work that "commemorates the tragic virtue of a pattern Victorian woman":

> Gaskell makes her [Charlotte Brontë] as immobile as an enchanted princess, an anguished servant of and martyr to her doomed and demanding family.[40]

Suzann Bick, too, idealizes Charlotte, comparing her to her mother.[41] Like Molly Gibson, Charlotte is portrayed as a virginal if "motherly friend and guardian to both [sisters] . . ." (111). Nursing the sick at home, Charlotte cancels visits to remain with her family, makes plans, and organizes the sisters' efforts to be published. Her manner is the quiet but subversive mode observed in Molly Gibson and Matty Jenkyns; she arranges for the publication of *Jane Eyre*, then breaks the news of its popular success quietly and indirectly to her father.

In separating Charlotte from her sisters and their passions, Gaskell minimizes her friend's rage, though traces of it seep into the descriptions of Brontë's restless nocturnal pacing. Gaskell further denies Brontë's anger by countering a letter from Charlotte signed "Caliban" (205) with another in which Brontë denies the validity of "intense *passion*, I am convinced that there is no desirable feeling . . ." (204). Gaskell notes, too, that for a time Brontë signed letters as "Charles Thunder," but she dismisses this claim to Jove's authority, commenting that Brontë was merely "making a kind of pseudonym for herself, out of her Christian name, and the meaning of her Greek surname." For Gaskell, such an assertion of anger and power could not be heartfelt; she refers to it as "assumed smartness" (202).

In contrast to Charlotte's repression, Emily strides about the moors and matches her dog's ferocity. Her unfashionably large sleeves render her conspicuous in Brussels, and her death is portrayed as a veritable battle with her body:

> Stronger than a man, simpler than a child, her nature stood alone. . . . on herself she had no pity; the spirit was inexorable to the flesh; from the trembling hands, the unnerved limbs, the fading eyes, the same service was exacted as they had rendered in health. (354)

Emily, all energy and vitality, can only destroy herself in her efforts to suppress the physical. Yet, in death, the physical is supremely dominant; it annihilates the spirit with itself.

Gaskell's depiction of Emily's death as a struggle between her and Charlotte illustrates that sisterly competition and friction have not been fully extinguished. Even in death, Emily "adhered tenaciously to her habits of independence. She would suffer no one to assist her" (356). Charlotte is excluded from Emily's battle with death; she cannot interfere, though her sister's funeral leaves her in almost unbearable solitude. Coral Lansbury has focused on the anger present at this time: "These are not the devoted sisters of sentimental fiction but two tragic women bound to each other by hostility as well as love."[42]

What are the sources of this hostility? Besides Charlotte's dependence on Emily for companionship, Gaskell emphasizes the rapidity with which Emily's decline follows Branwell's death. Indeed, by turning M. Héger into a father figure, Gaskell leaves Branwell as the brother-lover of the sister plot, the man over whom the women fight (as in *Cranford*, the closeness and inescapability of the family is emphasized by the fact that this figure *is* a biological brother). Charlotte's sorrow over leaving Héger is turned into grief over Branwell's dissipation, even though, in the process, Gaskell must "deliberately . . . antedate the disaster overtaking the brother, Branwell, which in fact did not occur till eighteen months later."[43] Branwell becomes the object of the women's subterfuges as they attempt to keep him away from drugs; like a lover, he becomes the focus of evasion and silence. Branwell's demise depletes Charlotte's energies, and his death, like Peter Jenkyns's escape, confirms and extends paternal power. With the subsequent deaths of Emily and Anne, Charlotte is bound irrevocably to remain with her father. Thus, the burials of Charlotte Brontë's siblings reinforce the prisonlike quality of the author's home.

Moreover, the passions that Emily has enacted for Charlotte are driven even further underground and into her fictions. Gaskell has not merely used Charlotte Brontë's sisters as a way of divorcing her from her anger; she has also dissociated her friend from her novels and heroines, passing over the publication of *Jane Eyre* with one sentence, explaining that "analysis" of the work is unnecessary because everyone has read it (36). In her uneasiness with Brontë's passions, Gaskell has divided Brontë the woman from Brontë the author, creating "two parallel currents" that resemble the split between sisters (334). Gaskell herself thus becomes a stand-in for patriarchal authority, a Deborah Jenkyns enforcing societal standards. Her careful maneuvering reveals Gaskell's own uncertainties about the manifestation of women's literary and sexual energies:

> Gaskell's depiction of Charlotte as the exemplar of conventional female virtue stems not only from her desire to separate Charlotte from her heroines, but also from Gaskell's own ambivalent response to the role of the creative process in woman's life.[44]

Ultimately then, Gaskell treats Brontë's texts as "ugly stepsisters," even as she adopts the role of the monitory sibling.

In reading this part of Gaskell's biography, one is struck by the depths of Brontë's depression, her frequent ill health and headaches, which appear to be physical manifestations of suppressed anger. Gaskell sees no release from these tensions in Brontë's marriage. Instead, Gaskell portrays Brontë as wearing away, still trapped at home, in a "marriage [that] secured papa good aid in his old age" (520). Conjugal life destroys her, and the woman so often depicted as being maternal dies giving birth. Gaskell could not have created a heavier irony if she had invented the whole story. Thus, in her biography as in her fiction, Gaskell leaves readers with an unsatisfying ending to the marriage plot. Her "heroine" suffers as much as a spinster as she does as a wife.

The end of the biography resembles the conclusions of her novels in other ways as well. Gaskell begins by portraying a relationship among blood sisters; she presents it as if it were part of a novel, stressing the difficulties and hardships in the sisters' lives. But, as in *Cranford* and *Wives and Daughters*, Gaskell ultimately offers an alternative fiction, a vision of sisterhood, in this case between herself and Charlotte Brontë. Her *Life* stands as a portrait of the sister Gaskell might have chosen, one whose similarities—but not her differences—are emphasized. As Yvonne Ffrench has commented, "temperamentally, they are both opposites,"[45] although readers of the biography might have trouble realizing this point, so effectively has Gaskell excised her friend's anger both in her depiction of her friend's life and in her neglect of her friend's works. Moreover, by stressing the importance of Ellen Nussey and Mary Taylor in Brontë's youth and by quoting their correspondence, Gaskell emphasizes the theme of sisterhood. In contrast, we are never allowed a full view of the Brontë parlor; we hear the girls' muffled pacing but not their conversation. Gaskell chooses to make our final view of the family one of two men at a cemetery, indicating that, as in *Cranford*, the patriarchy continues to dominate the sister story.

Gaskell pays homage to her friend-sister in *Cranford*, too, where the Brontës resurface in the Jenkyns sisters, reading their mother's love letters, shamed by their brother, and tyrannized by their father. Matty Jenkyns finds sisterhood with the narrator, who visits from the city, just as Gaskell comes to Charlotte Brontë from Manchester.

When Nina Auerbach writes about Gaskell's *Life of Charlotte Brontë*, she, too, acknowledges that the biography and *Cranford* are versions of the same story, noting that the pain of the "beleaguered [Brontë] sisters" has "seeped into and animated the genteel exclusiveness of Cranford. . . ."[46] But if the Jenkyns sisters are stand-ins for the Brontës, they and the men around them are altered and softened by the delicate allure of Gaskell's imagination. Auerbach cannot deny masculine strength in *The Life* with as much ease, nor can she ignore the importance of relationships among blood sisters. Consequently, she must detach herself (and her definition of reality) from Cranford, referring to it in the diminutive, as "little Cranford," from which "the outside world of masculinity, reality, and combat . . . remains a distanced and mysterious antagonist. . . ."[47] In her analysis of the biography, as in her discussion of the novella, Auerbach eventually "proclaims" a feminist reality based on a paradox: "The structure of the book suggests that the triumph of male reality is at one with its doom."[48] She enshrines the Brontë sisters, not as defeated martyrs, but as avenging furies, the Eumenides of Greek mythology, bent on haunting and conquering the men who survive them.

Against the haunting fury of a sister and the difficulty of separating one's self no matter how strongly one insists on viewing one's self as different, Gaskell consistently places the possibility of sisterhood, as an alternative, an act of choice. In *Cranford, Wives and Daughters,* and *The Life of Charlotte Brontë,* she contrasts relationships involving biological sisters, which are generated by the patriarchy, with bonds involving friendship, which are female creations. For Gaskell, sisterhood involves not competition but collusion in the subtle games of evasion pervading so much of women's communication.

Although it is tempting to perceive her vision as one that favors sisterhood and replaces the traditional sister story, in fact, sisterhood in Gaskell's books remains defined and threatened by the patriarchy. Her explorations of issues involving sisters and sisterhood are so significant that they reappear prominently in works by twentieth-century authors.

4

George Eliot
Superfluous Sisters

The Dodson sisters' constant criticism of each other's household economies, Celia Chettam's gossip with Mrs. Cadwallader about her sister's
possible remarriage, Gwendolen Harleth's scorn for her ignorant,
useless siblings—these illustrations from George Eliot's *Mill on the
Floss*, *Middlemarch*, and *Daniel Deronda* seem to belie any connection
between the words *sister* and *sisterhood*. At best, these women embody
clichés of female cattiness and petty competition; at worst, they remind readers of the archetypal sister story, "Cinderella."

Instead of being threatened by the possibility of never leaving home
or one another like Gaskell's heroines, Eliot's characters are uprooted,
scattered early in the novels by unwise marriages or financial reversals.
Open bickering replaces the veneer of politeness found in Austen's
works; Eliot's sisters often seem connected by nothing *but* blood, and
blood has little power.

Eliot herself had an ambivalent relationship with her sister Chrissey.
Although she assisted Chrissey in her domestic crises (of which there
were many), Eliot felt uncomfortable in her sister's household and was
hurt by her brother's interference in this relationship.[1] For the novelist, Chrissey represented the weakness of conventional femininity;
similar women populate Eliot's works, and the author's treatment of
these characters may reflect her reservations concerning her own
sister.

Eliot's distance from Chrissey may be apparent not only in the
hostility among her fictive siblings but also in sisters' relative unimpor-
tance in her narratives. Gwendolen Harleth's sisters remain faceless
and indistinguishable. The Dodsons, as aunts of the heroine, occupy a
marginal position in the narrative, even though they exert a great
influence over the Tullivers, and Celia Brooke resembles a stock figure
for much of *Middlemarch*, a foolish female absorbed with her baby,
fashions, and the superficial details of others' appearances. The rare
sisters who do get along with each other, such as the Meyricks in

Daniel Deronda, are even less developed than Celia. Their bonds to each other are not fully described; for instance, although the Gascoignes play a significant role in Gwendolen's life, Mrs. Davilow's relationship with Mrs. Gascoigne is sketchy at best. Many of the female siblings in Eliot's novels are so distanced that the texts scarcely seem to concern sisters at all.

The disloyalty among sisters dramatically sets off the social isolation of her unconventional heroines. Eliot finds no moral value in conforming to contemporary ideals and being a "good" sister. Even though Dorothea Brooke may be better than Maggie Tulliver's aunts, her superiority is not connected to her behavior as a sister, for she, too, can deliver a stinging retort or a pointed snub. She does not feel compelled, as Molly Gibson does in Gaskell's *Wives and Daughters*, to suppress anger or grief in her relationship with her sister. Indeed, Eliot's heroines are critical, if not harsh, toward their conforming sisters; they show none of Matty Jenkyns's deference to Deborah and the patriarchal code of Cranford. Ultimately, the distance between Eliot's sisters reflects the division between the heroine and society's expectations of her, or, to put it differently, conventional sisters (like Chrissey) come to represent society.

Although these women appear to have little use for each other, sisters in Eliot's works do serve stylistic and thematic functions. The siblings, who form complementary parts of one being, are opposites, but Eliot uses these polarities differently than Gaskell. Instead of concentrating on the sisters' dissimilarities and emphasizing the similarities in sisterhood, Eliot is concerned with the process by which sisters establish these differences, creating contrasts where few exist (both sisters, after all, are products of her imagination as well as occupants of virtually identical social positions). Her heroines consider themselves different from other women as well as from their sisters.

An earlier version of this process appears in *Pride and Prejudice* when Elizabeth and Lydia insist on their differences, even though both tend to be lively and outspoken. Whereas Austen's conclusion reinforces and confirms role divisions, Eliot questions them. She ultimately suggests that role splitting is an artifice, based on an illusory view of the self. Sisters are therefore intimately connected to Eliot's thematic focus on the multiple evasions of truth among Middlemarch residents.

The distinctions between sisters in Eliot's novels are also in perpetual flux. Eliot does not consistently assign qualities evenly among sisters, as Austen does. She creates an imbalance, so that one sister appears to have all the personality and the other none. This tactic heightens tension among sisters and undermines social expectations; as they renounce the fictive construct of "character," such women as Dorothea Brooke withdraw from female competition and reject traditionally sanctioned feminine behaviors. Yet, distancing, alienation, and separation all imply relationship, for one must be detached from something or someone. George Eliot's heroines' aspirations ultimately enmesh them further with society and their sisters. In coming to terms with her siblings, an Eliot heroine must confront society; she cannot be packed off, like Elizabeth Bennet in Austen's *Pride and Prejudice*, to a verdant, enclosed estate. Jenni Calder's description of the family in *The Mill on the Floss* as "dependent on an integral unity which it doesn't, cannot have"[2] summarizes the paradox involving sisters in *Daniel Deronda* and *Middlemarch* as well, a paradox that may be resolved best by Celia Brooke Chettam.

George Eliot's revisions of the sister plot are immediately evident in *The Mill on the Floss*. Even though the novel is more obviously a story of a brother and a sister, the Dodson sisters are instrumental in almost every major development. In the opening chapters of the book, for instance, Mr. Tulliver considers sending Tom to school, and Mrs. Tulliver calls in her siblings for advice. The move is as automatic as it is self-destructive; upon gaining the acquaintance of the daunting Aunt Glegg, the reader wonders why Mrs. Tulliver insists on consulting her.

The Dodsons' strife is a bitter caricature of sisterly behavior in Austen's novels, where marriage makes role splitting unnecessary by erecting barriers of class or geography. Even Aunt Norris's snobbery and manipulations in *Mansfield Park* are less damaging than the constant chorus of the Dodsons. Maggie's aunts remain locked in youthful competition; significantly, they consider themselves Dodsons and constantly point out Dodson traits in Tom.

An irony of *The Mill on the Floss* is that the Dodsons initially appear to embody the ideal of Victorian wifehood and sisterhood. Unlike Mary Barton's Aunt Esther, who is shunned because of her unconventional existence, the Dodsons are the very exemplars of conventionality. And while Esther is prevented from having much of an influence on her niece, the Dodson women are anything but distant; living in close proximity, they regularly visit and consult each other. Moreover, there is no lack of communication among them. They share village gossip, compare one another's housekeeping and economies, and show off their prized possessions. When Maggie returns from her escape with Stephen Guest, Aunt Glegg offers shelter as evidence of familial solidarity.

Such intimacy, however, is as illusory as Aunt Glegg's false "fronts" of glossy curls,[3] for the Dodsons as a group before the public treat one another far differently than they do in private: "While no individual Dodson was satisfied with any other individual Dodson, each was satisfied, not only with him or herself, but with the Dodsons collectively" (97). The public face, the Dodsons "collectively," is the vestige of an intimate family. Its sterility is evident in the fact that only two of the sisters have children, and Mrs. Tulliver and Mrs. Deane's three offspring combined are no match for Aunt Moss's brood of eight.

Similarly, meaningful family rituals, such as the excitement of the Bennets at having a male guest to dinner or Molly Gibson's accompanying her father on his rounds, have been replaced by petty rules. Although these regulations might once have served a purpose, their only remaining function is to remind the women of their superiority:

> There were particular ways of doing everything in that family: particular ways of bleaching the linen, of making the cowslip wine, curing the hams and keeping the bottled gooseberries, so that no daughter of that house could be indifferent to the privilege of having been born a Dodson, rather than a Gibson, or Watson. (96)

The Dodsons' household rules create illusory distinctions, for readers are given no evidence that "that family" is indeed any different from the Gibsons or Watsons, and the similarity in names implies that other resemblances might exist as well. Moreover, the emptiness of family forms is apparent in the fact that so many of them pertain to death. Mrs. Tulliver shows her love for her husband by saving the best sheets for his shroud. Her sensuality has been channeled into the futile anticipation of the texture of the linens "mangled beautiful, an' all ready, an' smell o' lavender" (58) next to their corpses. "Funerals were always conducted with peculiar propriety in the Dodson family" (96)—appropriately, as Nina Auerbach has noted, "Given their tendency to embalm life's crises in layers of ritual. . . ."[4]

Ritual and propriety, like the padding on Aunt Pullet's precious bonnet, protect the Dodsons from any show of genuine compassion or warmth (even the display of Aunt Pullet's hat, which could be a lighthearted event, is treated with "funereal solemnity," 150). The frequent visits mask stinginess, not only with money but also with affection. The Dodsons will help the impoverished Tullivers only if they will be chastened and "humble . . . in mind" (290). Similarly, Aunt Glegg will take in Maggie if she will affect the proper humility (631). Utterly self-serving, she anticipates praise for her generosity and preservation of family unity, even as she expects to benefit from Maggie's "dutiful" (631) household assistance. Aunt Glegg's convenient offer thus reminds Maggie that her aunt's greatest pride is her economy; Mrs. Glegg lives by the platitude "waste not, want not," refusing to acknowledge the waste that will occur if she dies with her best lace untouched.

In a similar situation, Austen's Fanny Price is admitted to the community at Mansfield Park at the urging of her selfish Aunt Norris. Although Fanny, too, occupies an equivocal position in the household, she is slowly allowed to take part in family rituals and activities, culminating in the ball (reminiscent of the one in "Cinderella") at which she is the center of attention. Her admission to the family is confirmed when she marries Edmund Bertram, and Aunt Norris, who would keep Fanny subservient, is banished along with Maria Bertram.

The Dodsons are so rigidly entrenched in their attitudes that such changes would be unimaginable to them. Furthermore, they are oblivious to the paradoxes inherent in their actions, as when Aunt Glegg's hoarding to prevent waste ultimately creates it. They are unconscious of the irony that their defensive behavior is destructive. Whereas marriage separates Austen's sisters in terms of class and geography, the Dodsons, with the exception of Bessie Tulliver, occupy similar positions in the social hierarchy of St. Ogg's. They must, therefore, constantly assert their individuality by emphasizing their differences from and superiority to their sisters. This is a private version of the Dodsons' "collective" snobbery in town; as separate human beings, the Dodsons exist primarily to antagonize one another. Aunt Pullet's elaborate preparations for the Tullivers' visit, for instance, are calculated not only to preserve her possessions but also to draw attention to their value. Implicit in Aunt Pullet's behavior is criticism of her sister Tulliver for having such careless children. Just as Aunt Pullet's pride is her home, Aunt Glegg's is her parsimony, and Aunt Deane's is Lucy. Each has her territory staked out, including Mrs. Tulliver, who was selected by Mr. Tulliver for her good looks and stupidity (68).

Among themselves, the sisters squabble and take sides to protect their territories. Kindness is so rare that when Aunt Glegg offers to harbor Maggie, Mrs. Tulliver notes with surprise that her sibling is behaving "like a sister" (631). More often, the excess chatter exists only to humiliate or educate, and at the most trying times:

> When one of the family was in trouble or sickness, all the rest went to visit the unfortunate member, usually at the same time, and did not shrink from uttering the most disagreeable truths that correct family feeling dictated. . . . (96–97)

The Dodsons pretend that "family feeling" is not a matter of emotion but of correctness or incorrectness; exhibiting it properly (i.e., hurting others) is a duty. Indeed, like Deborah Jenkyns in Gaskell's *Cranford,* the sisters gain power by assuming the authority of convention and outperforming each other in propriety.

When the sisters ally themselves against the Tullivers under the guise of being helpful, the Dodson chorus becomes the voice of authority, of the society they try to control with their ossified standards. Mrs. Tulliver reveals the Dodsons' true importance when she glides from speaking of her sisters to "folks" as if they were the same:

> I'll tell your aunt Glegg and aunt Pullet when they come next week, and they'll never love you any more. O dear, O dear, look at your clean pinafore, wet from top to bottom. Folks 'ull think it's a judgment on me as I've got such a child—they'll think I've done summat wicked. (78)

The Dodsons, with their arcane rituals, collect to judge other women and discourage nonconformity as if it were a moral lapse. It is no wonder, then, that as a child Maggie feels desperate enough to escape their censure; an outcast from the family, she considers herself alienated from the entire community.

The Dodsons' behavior has another effect, too. Lucy and Maggie are often thought to be like sisters (563, 620), and the aunts constantly compare the cousins, to Maggie's disadvantage. In this way, the Dodsons prepare for their rivalry to be perpetuated in the next generation. And they succeed. Without models of womanly solidarity or sisterhood, Maggie has little cause to feel compunction for running away with Stephen Guest.

The Dodsons thus play a significant role in *The Mill on the Floss.* They are responsible for Maggie's becoming acquainted with Stephen Guest (through the Deanes) as well as for Mr. Tulliver's fatal loan. But most of all, George Eliot's portrayal of the occasionally ridiculous family of sisters lays the groundwork for her treatment of sisters in later novels. Mrs. Tulliver's surprise when Mrs. Glegg acts "like a sister" is evidence of the slippage between the idealized meaning of the term *sister* inherited from patriarchal conventions and its applied meaning in the siblings' lives. While Molly Gibson struggles valiantly to overcome this slippage, to live up to her understanding of the word, the discrepancy in the definitions becomes increasingly noticeable in George Eliot's works as well as in the twentieth-century novels that will be discussed in the last two chapters of this study.

In *Middlemarch,* sisters play a significant part, too, although their relationship initially appears marginal in Eliot's larger design. The plot of the novel is instigated by a spat between sisters. As Celia and

Dorothea sort their mother's jewels, Dorothea asserts her individuality as the intellectual, unworldly sister, but not with complete success. In fact, it is in part *because* Celia catches her sibling admiring jewels that Dorothea finds herself attracted to Casaubon; she must defend her difference.

The debate over the jewels introduces an abbreviated version of the sister plot. Eliot shows the destructive effects of one sister's attachment to a father figure in Dorothea's first marriage. When Sir James Chettam rapidly transfers his affection from Dorothea to Celia, just as Mr. Collins offers his hand to Charlotte Lucas after Elizabeth Bennet rejects him, Eliot reminds readers of the sisters' social equivalence. Eliot also provides Will Ladislaw as a brother-lover; Casaubon's will initially acts with the force of an incest taboo (and indeed Dorothea rationalizes her interest in Will as legitimate concern for a member of her husband's family). Her recognition of Will as a lover and potential spouse, as with Fanny Price and Molly Gibson, occurs only after Dorothea fears that she has lost him to a rival. Finally, marriage erects social barriers between the sisters.

This skeletal summary of the plot illustrates the marginality of the sister story in *Middlemarch*. Eliot is preoccupied with larger plotting; to the extent that she focuses on sisters, she is concerned with their shifting interactions as they strive to differentiate. The traditional role splitting and alliances work no better for the Brookes in *Middlemarch* than they do for the Dodsons in *The Mill on the Floss*.

Neither sisters nor sisterhood provides much solace for the isolated Dorothea. The town chorus of Mrs. Cadwallader and her friends constantly judges Dorothea, wonders about her life and her choices, and ultimately "cuts" her socially. Instead of quietly supporting her efforts to be independent, as the women of Cranford covertly aid Matty Jenkyns, the women of Middlemarch are afraid of their neighbor's unconventionality, taking it as implicit criticism of their own lives. The novelistic convention of the sister plot also isolates Dorothea as it erects barriers between her and Celia. When the two sisters talk, they do not necessarily communicate; rather, each is trying to educate the other, to convert her to her own style of life. Finally, in examining sisterly relations and urging readers to take sides, Eliot forces her audience to evaluate conventions and their failures.

From the first pages of the book, Celia and Dorothea appear to exhibit opposite personal qualities. Celia is commonsensical, while her sister aspires to higher ideals. However, the contrast's sole purpose is not the banal one of introducing character. Many readers feel challenged to side with one sister or the other, to commit to one view of life to the exclusion of the other.

Reading commentaries on *Middlemarch*, one notices how rapidly critics make such a commitment. Their opinions tend to extremes, as if one's reaction to Dorothea Brooke held all the import of a political stance (which, in some ways, it does). Ellen Moers's description of Dorothea might equally be applied to Rosamond Vincy or Gwendolen Harleth at their vainest, so negatively does she judge Dorothea:

> She is good at nothing *but* to be admired. . . . Ignorant in the extreme and mentally idle . . . Dorothea has little of interest to say, but a magnificent voice to say it in.

Moers's bitterness belies an expectation of a more noble heroine, perhaps one who might live up to Nina Auerbach's ideal of sisterhood. Indeed, almost as often as they take sides, critics and other readers express feelings of betrayal. Lee Edwards begins, "I saw in Dorothea an endorsement . . . of energy and social commitment on the part of a woman," and ends with disappointment, "For *Middlemarch* is finally not an endorsement of this energy, but . . . a condemnation of it." Patricia Beer acknowledges a different dissatisfaction, finding Celia at first "a sympathetic character," although she is later troubled by Celia's "malice" and must seek motives to justify her behavior.[5] How is it that Dorothea, who initially appears a visionary (albeit with priggish instincts), becomes "poor Dorothea," and Celia, who is so practical, comes to resemble a caricature of a doting mother? How and why does Eliot shift the terms of the contrast during the novel so that it is difficult and uncomfortable to side unequivocally with one sister?

Repeatedly, critics refer to Celia as Dorothea's "foil,"[6] emphasizing the polarization of the two sisters. The same term was used by critics to describe the characterization of the Dashwood sisters in *Sense and Sensibility*. In this case, the various meanings of *foil* offer a fuller understanding of the complexity of Celia's role. A foil can be an obstacle or an obstruction—which Celia initially appears—and also a defensive weapon. Although the former seems opposed to the latter, both apply to Celia as she is viewed from shifting perspectives.

The opening scene of the novel illustrates how Eliot constantly alters the terms of the contrast between Celia and Dorothea, or, to use one of her metaphors, moves the pier glass. The reader, prepared by the introduction to view Dorothea as an exceptional woman, is confronted in the first sentence with a completely conventional perspective: "Miss Brooke had that kind of beauty which seems to be thrown into relief by poor dress" (1). The heroine is presented as an object to be admired; that is all. The narrator then compares Dorothea's clothing to "provincial fashion" and sets up an opposition between the sisters: "[Dorothea] was usually spoken of as being remarkably clever, but with the addition that her sister Celia had more common-sense" (1). In the minds of the unidentified speakers, the sisters are insepara- ble; they cannot refer to Dorothea without mentioning her sibling. "The addition" to the sentence implies that the word *clever* is being used sarcastically, and that the speakers prefer Celia. So far, Dorothea seems anything but exceptional, and the next sentence confuses the discussion still further:

> Nevertheless, Celia wore scarcely more trimmings; and it was only to close observers that her dress differed from her sister's, and had a shade of coquetry in its arrangements; for Miss Brooke's plain dressing was due to mixed conditions, in most of which her sister shared. (1)

The first half of the sentence implies that Dorothea, far from being a potential saint, is hardly different from her sister. Dorothea's apparel is not the result of intellectual, moral or religious convictions; it is due to "mixed conditions" shared by Celia. In the next part of the sen- tence, the speaker veers away, criticizing Celia, but in the end the narrator reminds us of the similarity of the sisters' lots.

The opening of the novel is ambiguous. If the differences between the sisters are not immediately apparent, do they in fact exist? If they do exist, are the differences great enough to be significant? Is Dor- othea's character morally superior to Celia's, and the character of an aspiring Saint Theresa? Or are the sisters' differences products of their imaginations? Who are the "close observers," and what is their au- thority? Obviously, some of these questions, especially those con- cerning authority, could be asked of any novel; here, as with Lydia and Elizabeth Bennet, the reader is led to wonder not only about the characters' personalities, but also about the validity of the distinctions between them.

The remainder of the chapter is scarcely more enlightening. Throughout, the girls' statements and gestures can be interpreted in more than one way. For instance, Celia remarks petulantly (and point- edly) that Dorothea has kept their mother's jewels exactly six months (5). Dorothea laughs in response; given Celia's mortification, one must assume that this laughter expresses sarcasm as well as sympathy. Similarly, Dorothea's "air of astonished discovery" (5) could be an example of Miss Brooke's famous blindness or coyness (coming from Celia, the request is anything but astonishing). And Dorothea's con- sternation as she "seemed to despair of her memory" (5) is also questionable, because she has near perfect recall of her duties and studies. The terms *air* and *seemed* undercut Dorothea's candor; is she merely making her sister squirm? The episode itself has the tone of a set piece, a kind of performance the sisters have undertaken dozens of times, complete with Celia's prepared rationalization, "necklaces are quite usual now," and effective "rising sob" (5).

The studied quality of the conversation suggests that the women's behavior, like that of the Dodson sisters, has become ritualized. In this case, the routine allows Dorothea to make "a strong assumption of superiority" (6) quite unsupported by her actions, especially when she accepts the emeralds. Celia plays the victim whose "blond flesh" feels "a Puritanic persecution" (6). Despite the occasional spiteful remark, her opposition remains covert:

> Since they could remember, there had been a mixture of criticism and awe in the attitude of Celia's mind towards her elder sister. The younger had always worn a yoke; but is there any yoked creature without its opinions? (7)

Later, the balance shifts. Dorothea appears on the defensive as she must bear Celia's remarks about Casaubon's moles, eating habits, and general demeanor. Celia's mode of communication remains covert, however, as she attempts to warn Dorothea of Casaubon's sterility.

No matter how carefully distinctions are established, they collapse, and conventional role divisions cannot be maintained. Dorothea suppresses her sensuality, but it still exists; she rejects Sir James Chettam's offer of a horse, though she has enjoyed cantering. Dorothea tries valiantly to be a "good," dutiful wife and woman, but she acknowledges wistfully to Will that Celia "never was naughty in her life" (52), implying that she, Dorothea, has been "naughty."

Nevertheless, a pattern emerges, as the narrator becomes detached from the "speakers" and "observers" of Middlemarch. Dorothea is supported by the narrator, because she has high aspirations and must suffer their frustration. Celia is favored by the authorities of the community (Mr. Brooke, Sir James, and Mrs. Cadwallader), because she poses less of a threat to their standards. Ranged with the town's leaders, Celia, like the Dodson sisters, becomes a representative of the society that restricts Dorothea (and the reader, too, must choose between the narrator's view and Middlemarch's predilection). Celia is empowered not only by her own position, but also by Dorothea's practice of self-abnegation.

Dorothea perceives marriage as an opportunity for self-sacrifice. She makes her life a long series of renunciations: of finery, personal aspirations, and dreams of conjugal companionship. Envisioning herself dutifully taking orders from her husband, she considers her unwillingness to fulfill Casaubon's dying wish her greatest failure. Dorothea believes that goodness involves an emptying of personality, a giving up of will (and, for a time, Will), even though such self-denial is painful. Ultimately, although Moers's remark that Dorothea "does little but harm in the novel"[7] may be an exaggeration, there is no question that Dorothea accomplishes little of what she intended, "absorbed in the life of another, and . . . only known in a certain circle as a wife and mother" (576).

On the other hand, Celia, who is not the heroine of the novel, becomes increasingly assertive. As Dorothea affects meekness, Celia grows strong and judgmental, and, once she has a child, Celia claims authority over her sister. Her silliness and submission are protective cover. Although Robert Coles portrays Celia as the traditionally passive, dominated Victorian woman,[8] Celia is ultimately able to manipulate her husband, her sister, and others. Her achievement is yet another reversal of the expectations created by the Prelude. Celia defends her sister and smooths her way, behaving as a protective foil even when it is not to her advantage (as when she encourages Dorothea to consider a second marriage, even though little Arthur might then lose the opportunity to inherit Mr. Brooke's estate). When Dorothea does remarry, Celia brings her back into the family: "Such being the bent of Celia's heart, it was inevitable that Sir James should consent to a reconciliation with Dorothea and her husband. Where women love each other, men learn to smother their dislike" (577).

By the end of the novel, each woman offers an alternative to traditional role splitting among sisters. Dorothea has attempted to renounce personality. Although she has ostensibly gained a vision of common humanity following her confrontation with Will and Rosamond, Dorothea continues to separate herself from others and to disparage Celia's capabilities. In fact, Dorothea's final words in the novel, which are addressed to her sister, suggest narrowness more than universal sympathy: "You would have to feel with me, else you would never know" (567). On the other hand, Celia's apparent stupidity—her belief that she can indeed "know" what Dorothea feels—empowers her. What Celia learns is that, despite her sister's denials, Dorothea shares many of her feelings, such as the sensual pleasure in an exquisite gem and the desire to marry a lively young suitor. As Dorothea retreats from personality, Celia absorbs it, accepting her sister's traits.

In *Middlemarch*, as in *The Mill on the Floss*, Eliot suggests that the traditional division of roles among sisters is inadequate. Instead of suppressing sisterly animosities, as Elizabeth Gaskell does in her biography of Charlotte Brontë, Eliot emphasizes them, forcing readers to accept that sisters can behave in hurtful ways. Moreover, role splitting leads to an illusory (because limited) view, as when Dorothea ignores Celia's real accomplishments. To gain a fuller vision, a woman must give up competition. She must acknowledge that she is a part of, not apart from, the world of women.

By presenting this theme as a problem in reading in *Middlemarch*, George Eliot adds another dimension to the work. The reader of Austen's *Sense and Sensibility* must participate in the sisterly process of differentiation, too, but toward another end. Austen's goal is to show how role splitting involves denying a part of one's self; in contrast, Eliot questions the notion of self altogether. Eliot's reader, like her characters, must confront preconceptions about personality as well as conventional assumptions of what constitutes "good" sisterly behavior.

Daniel Deronda provides an even more negative view of sisters and sisterhood than *Middlemarch*. Gwendolen Harleth's silly, ignorant siblings are as irritating to her as the Dodsons are to Maggie Tulliver; when Gwendolen's family loses its money, the gravity of the predicament is increased by the number of mouths to be fed. Gwendolen perceives her sisters primarily as an obstacle, a source of misery in her life, keeping her "a princess in exile"[9] from the special fate she believes to be hers. Her sisters' very existence convinces her that "girls' lives are stupid: they never do anything they like" (101). Unaccomplished and utterly conventional, the girls are paralyzed by catastrophe: "Your poor sisters can only cry . . . and give . . . no help" (44).

Whereas Molly Gibson in Gaskell's *Wives and Daughters* wishes to accept her stepsister as a biological sibling, Gwendolen Harleth feels no kinship with her half sisters, who are in fact blood relatives. She hates the younger girls because, even more than Lydia Glasher, the "superfluous" (611) siblings represent "a woman's life" (190) restricted by society. In *Pride and Prejudice*, Elizabeth Bennet is more comfortable in the study than in the kitchen, but she feels neither horror nor claustrophobia when contemplating the female sphere. Her detached irony is milder than Gwendolen Harleth's utter repulsion. When Gwendolen's half sister Isabel leaves a hidden panel unlatched, she terrifies Gwendolen with its depiction of an "obscure" figure fleeing death. Isabel has exposed the futility of Gwendolen's attempt to escape a traditional woman's existence (56), and Gwendolen cannot bear it.

In fact, Gwendolen, like Dorothea, resembles other women and shares their fate. She must contrive elaborate tactics to persuade herself otherwise; among them, "Gwendolen shuns her own sex, girls

like her who reflect her own insignificance."[10] She detests her sisters
because they reveal her own superfluity and lack of accomplishments.
She is only marginally more proficient than they are, and her age
rather than her superior talents may account for this difference.
Gwendolen's sole significant advantage over her sisters is her beauty;
consequently, she is determined to use it in creating her future. The
fear of "a woman's life," as embodied in her sisters, thus precipitates
Gwendolen's story.

Initially, the role splitting in *Daniel Deronda*, which allows Gwendolen to insist on being different and superior, seems rather rudimen-
tary: Gwendolen has all the personality, and her half sisters have none.
As in *Middlemarch*, the sister plot is abbreviated and disastrous.
Without a father, Gwendolen allies herself with her uncle and takes
over at home, having "usurped the man's position in relation to her
mother."[11] She orders her mother about and is alienated from the
women around her: "Gwendolen was not a general favourite with her
own sex . . ." (150). Instead of accepting her cousin Rex, who lives so
close as to be a brotherly suitor, she perceives the limitations of his
life. Aspiring to social heights and feeling no attraction, she refuses his
offer. She prefers to wed the paternal Grandcourt, although the match
is a catastrophe. Gwendolen finds herself uprooted, and she is rejected
by Deronda, who becomes another brotherly figure in his helpfulness
and denial of any romantic relation between them. The features of the
traditional sister plot thus offer Gwendolen no happiness or concluding marriage with a brother-lover.

George Eliot's vision of sisters in *Daniel Deronda* is more concentrated and pessimistic than in *Middlemarch*. She provides no Celia
figure, no well-developed alternative to Gwendolen's isolation. Mirah,
potentially a surrogate sister, is friendly with the Meyrick girls (even
as she deprives them of the object of their affections), but she is awed
by and uncomfortable with other women. Although Catherine Arrow-
point is kind to Gwendolen, the heroine is ill at ease with the heiress's
genuine artistry and altruism.

The Meyricks initially appear to offer an alternative to Gwendolen's
alienation from her sisters and peers, presenting a positive model of
sisterly behavior. After taking second place to a brother all their lives,
they are conscious of being "of minor importance in the world . . ."
(717). Having fewer illusions than Gwendolen about a young woman's
social position, they work together instead of competing for recognition.

On the other hand, as a reflection of the heroine's trio of half sisters,
the Meyricks are poor and socially redundant; they further resemble
the "superfluous" siblings in their almost complete lack of individu-

ality. Readers find it difficult to distinguish between Amy and Mab, for instance. The Meyricks get along so well that they appear to be caricatures of idealized sisterly intimacy, and one wonders whether Eliot's intention in including them in the novel is ironic. Moreover, because the Meyricks have never separated, they have difficulty accepting the individuality of nonbiological siblings. Embroidering stories around Mirah as if she were a character in a romance, they appropriate her life. They revere the stately Gwendolen, considering her an artifact to be appreciated (and significantly, their brother refers to her as the "Vandyke Duchess," 707). Transforming the lives of other women, the diminutive, impish Meyricks resemble fairies, and, in fact, Mab bears a fairy's name. The Meyricks are in an authorial (and readerly) position, creating the sisters they desire. In doing so, they neglect to develop their own identities or to establish a genuine sisterhood with peers.

In the end, Eliot offers no completely positive view of sisterly behavior. She allows Gwendolen no foil, no constructed character against whom she may define her identity. Rather, in confronting her ordinariness, Gwendolen must realize her similarity to her sisters. Thus *Daniel Deronda* is ultimately no fairy-tale world; the novel is replete with threesomes and foursomes, but no special child emerges to win the prize, because all the offspring are essentially the same:

> There is a daunting superfluity of women in *Daniel Deronda:* three Meyrick girls, three Mallinger girls, three illegitimate Grandcourt daughters, Gwendolen's sisters, and the three Mompert girls she is almost engaged to teach. Gwendolen's sense of distinction is understandably uncommon.[12]

As much as Gwendolen's sense of privilege is "uncommon," it is also undeserved, as she rapidly learns.

Daniel Deronda shows the futility and falsity of distinctions between sisters; furthermore, it illustrates how the desire for recognition isolates and nearly destroys Gwendolen, stifling much of the warmth in her nature. In the final chapters of the novel, Gwendolen sees herself not as the heroine of a Byronic "romance" (774), too proud to acknowledge her sorrows, but as a human being. She longs to see her "troublesome sisters coming out [of their house] to meet her" (831), and, as Bonnie Zimmerman notes, "her final acceptance of her mother and stepsisters represents her final acceptance of the woman within herself, an acceptance that has both positive and negative implications." These implications are mixed because in some ways her recognition constitutes a "retreat to the womb"[13] and undifferentiation.

To improve, Gwendolen must be stripped of many of her impulses and much of what has constituted her character; she must allow more space for her sisters' growth. Her development thus parallels Dorothea's more than Celia's. Her sisters, too, must change. They can no longer treat Gwendolen as an awesome, distant heroine. Instead of being dependent, passive spectators in their sister's life, they must live for themselves, though nowhere does Eliot describe what their lives might be. Presumably, they remain socially redundant.

At the end of *Daniel Deronda*, as in the conclusion of *Middlemarch*, the heroine and her siblings are forced to revise their self-perceptions. But in the later novel, George Eliot signals no greater happiness or achievement because of these altered views. Gwendolen's subdued personality has little force or significance in the world of the novel, even though she asserts that she will be "better" (882). Gwendolen's change can only be effective on a different level, that of the reader, who, as in *Middlemarch*, must first participate in and then renounce the heroine's aspirations to a special fate.

George Eliot's treatment of the sister theme is thus more pessimistic than in the earlier novels I have discussed. Eliot goes beyond Austen and Gaskell, for whom role splitting serves certain beneficial purposes even if characters must deny parts of themselves. For Eliot, role splitting is an ossified ritual that cripples sisters, forcing them to overlook their similarities. It never succeeds in eliminating competition; instead, the sisters in Eliot's novels are so insecure that they continually attempt to assert their superiority over one another, even after marriage. Ultimately, the distinctions that define character are revealed to be fictive and destructive.

In her later novels, Eliot allows her characters some insight into the damage caused by role splitting, as Celia Brooke and Gwendolen Harleth begin to accept their commonalities with other women, and to adopt an inclusive notion of their own personalities. However, these are small realizations with little power or effect in the women's communities.

Eliot's greatest contribution to our understanding of the sister story is on the reader's level. Austen maintains the fictive convention of the happy ending by providing an often strained conclusion that reinforces sisterly divisions along class and geographic barriers. She reveals how role splitting involves denying part of the self, but she sees the process as a necessary part of maturation. Gaskell, on the other hand, participates in the sister story in her *Life of Charlotte Brontë*, inserting herself in the place of biological siblings. This technique allows her, too, to maintain the convention of harmony among "good" women. In her work, the friction among blood kin is suppressed as she offers an alternative vision of sisterhood based on similarity instead of difference. Eliot follows the others' lead in treating sisterly issues beyond the plot level. She encourages her audience to participate in the sisterly game of role splitting and to understand the cramping, binding quality of this convention, in which sisters are forced to overlook their similarities.

Eliot's examination of role splitting and her portrayal of its dangers are useful in our study of later novels. Characters in twentieth-century novels, like those in Eliot's fictions, must confront the impossibility of maintaining role distinctions in a world where definitions of identity, character, and women's roles begin to shift in a rapid and often perplexing manner.

5

Pym, Howard, and Drabble
Revising the Sister

Compared to two of the twentieth century's most popular depictions of sisters, *Gone with the Wind* and *Whatever Happened to Baby Jane* (both more famous as films than as printed texts), Gwendolen Harleth's distaste for her siblings and gender in Eliot's *Daniel Deronda* appears trivial. Although George Eliot addresses the hostility between biological sisters more explicitly than her predecessors, later women novelists further expose the gap between biological siblings' behavior and ideals of sisterhood (although many of these texts, too, pale in comparison to the works mentioned above). This disparity has preoccupied such diverse authors as Rebecca West, May Sinclair, Margaret Drabble, Barbara Pym, Elizabeth Jane Howard, Elizabeth Taylor, Emma Tennant, and Doris Lessing as they have struggled to come to terms with the shifting position of women in society. Like Elizabeth Gaskell before them, these women react as readers as well as writers in their treatment of the topic, commenting on nineteenth-century sister stories.

Barbara Pym, Margaret Drabble, and Elizabeth Jane Howard, writing toward the middle of the twentieth century, are particularly concerned with sisters and sisterhood. For instance, Harriet and Belinda Bede, the heroines of Barbara Pym's first novel, *Some Tame Gazelle*, are modeled on the author and her sister. The Bedes reappear in her later work, *An Unsuitable Attachment*, which features another pair of sisters as well. In her first novel, *A Summer Bird-Cage*, Margaret Drabble seeks to resolve sibling conflicts, and in *After Julius* Elizabeth Jane Howard portrays a mother and two daughters confronting not only the men in their lives but also one another, as the traditional love triangle of heterosexual romances is replaced by a triad of women. None of these novels is particularly experimental structurally; all have continuous, linear plots. Instead of making major innovations in plot or theme, the authors reexamine issues that have appeared often in novels about sisters and raise critical questions about relationships among women.

Specifically, these texts are about the connections between contemporary novelists and their predecessors as well as their works. The authors of these novels treat earlier writers as older sisters, at once emulating them, paying homage, and struggling to break away from their influence. May Sinclair's novel, *The Three Sisters*, for instance, is a revision of Gaskell's *Life of Charlotte Brontë* that fully reveals the destructive nature of patriarchal repression. In their intertextuality, such works confront issues of sisterhood, even as within their plots they deal with biological siblings. Thus, these more contemporary novels constitute an appropriate basis for a discussion of the slippage from one term to the other and the merging of the two relationships in the minds of critics, who are authors themselves.

Repeatedly, writers name their characters after heroines in other books; the surname of the speaker in *A Summer Bird-Cage* is Bennett, and a character in *After Julius* was baptized Emma. Although literary allusions are not limited to nineteenth-century stories about sisters (Emma's promiscuous sibling is called Cressida, and one of the sisters in *An Unsuitable Attachment* is named Penelope Grandison), Austen's novels are the source of a disproportionately large number of names.

Direct references to novels concerning sisters are made, too, as when the mother in *After Julius* rereads *Pride and Prejudice*. Robert Long and Margaret Ezell have noticed resemblances among the heroines of *Some Tame Gazelle* and *Cranford*, while, for Gail Cunningham, "*A Summer Bird-Cage*, with its neatly wrought comparisons and contrasts of marriage types, inevitably recalls *Pride and Prejudice*. . . ."[1] A scene in *A Summer Bird-Cage* reflects on *Middlemarch* as well. The heroine's sister Louise is seen honeymooning in Rome, all dressed in gray and "posed expensively against an artistic background,"[2] which resembles the setting of Will Ladislaw's encounter with Dorothea in Rome.

Drabble, Pym, and Howard also pay homage to their predecessors by featuring elements of the traditional sister plot. In each text, sisters' roles are laboriously divided. The women criticize each other gently or compete bitterly. In *Some Tame Gazelle*, a lover, Theo Grote, transfers his allegiance from one sister to the other, and then to a third woman, recalling in part Sir James Chettam in Eliot's *Middlemarch*, as well as Wickham and Mr. Collins in Austen's *Pride and Prejudice*. A character in *After Julius* is considered "brotherly"[3] by the heroine before she accepts him as a lover, while her sister forms an attachment to a father figure.

In some cases, the authors' admiration for their predecessors has been openly declared. Pym, for instance, acknowledged that she especially enjoyed reading Austen. Margaret Drabble has stated on several occasions her respect for George Eliot as well as for Elizabeth Gaskell.[4]

However, the allusions are, as often as not, ironic or based on deliberately illusory interpretations of the nineteenth-century novels. The authors do not merely intend to pay homage; as Sandra Gilbert and Susan Gubar have indicated, they are "relating to . . . [their] lineage . . . through the creation of parodic and allusive texts—novels, stories, and plays that function quasi-critically and refer to or revise female pre-texts."[5] Thus, Drabble's Louise may resemble Dorothea Brooke on her honeymoon in Rome, but Louise is also openly adulterous and mercenary. In making her Emma shy, passive and silent, Elizabeth Jane Howard complicates her allusion not only to Austen's heroine but also to Flaubert's Madame Bovary. And in *A Summer Bird-Cage,* the heroine compares a rare instance of intimacy with her sister to the politeness of an Austen novel or *Middlemarch* (171), conveniently forgetting the behavior of such sisters as Maria Bertram, Lydia Bennet, and Elizabeth Elliott, not to mention the bickering between Dorothea and Celia Brooke. The references to nineteenth-century novels are placed before the reader's eyes, tantalizing, like signposts to positive significance, only to swivel in the opposite direction or to mislead the unwary.

Indeed, the authors are as inconsistent in their statements regarding their predecessors as they are in their use of allusions. According to Janice Rossen, Pym felt ambivalent about being compared to Austen, finding the latter's work "an impossibly high standard to attain."[6] Drabble has repeatedly criticized Austen in interviews, asserting that Austen shares the negative qualities of Louise in *A Summer Bird-Cage:* "I think she's a pernicious and terrible influence, Jane Austen, sort of malicious and exclusive and socially unjust, really."[7] Yet, despite Drabble's well-documented and often-cited distaste for Austen's work, it appears that the twentieth-century writer has moderated her dislike. In an interview at the 1988 Modern Language Association convention, Drabble reiterated her conviction that the portrayals of Elizabeth and Jane Bennet in *Pride and Prejudice* are "idealized," but commented that, as she rereads Austen, her opinion of the nineteenth-century author grows more positive. She expressed particular sympathy for Mary, who is left out of many of the family interactions, wondering how the story might differ if written from Mary's point of view.[8]

Such mixed emotions and shifting viewpoints suggest that twentieth-century authors treat their predecessors not only as influential literary mothers but also as literary siblings and rivals. Their works concern their relationships to other authors as well as the dilemmas of fictional siblings, and, in this sense, they owe a great deal to Gaskell's *Life of Charlotte Brontë*. Finally, these writers seek not only an appropriate voice for certain issues in their own time, but also to come to terms with issues that persist across time.

The intertextuality of these novels is even more apparent when one considers the infrequency of references to myths and tales concerning sisters. Cinderella and Psyche are rarely alluded to directly or indirectly; at best, the myths and tales are ambiguous models, and at worst, they are irrelevant. These authors may be writing about events involving sisters because, as Margaret Drabble has pointed out, "they're just archetypal situations,"[9] but most of the types come from female adaptations of patriarchal plots. Masculine texts are brought up only to be criticized, swept aside, or replaced.

If the traditional sister plot no longer fits Eliot's world, it is even less suited to the twentieth century, where marriage is less likely to be the primary concern of spinster sisters living alone. Nevertheless, recent texts value certain conventions. All contain shadows (at least) of a traditional courtship plot, even as they search for alternatives. Specifically, in depicting their heroines, the authors are divided: how can they create a sexual, unrepressed character, appropriate to twentieth-century standards, and keep her a conventionally "good" girl, quiet, submissive, and possibly headed for the altar? How can they rebel against their literary predecessors and yet satisfy certain conventions? Coming to terms with these questions involves bringing sisterly conflicts to the forefront:

> In *Pride and Prejudice* the relationship of the sisters to one another is peripheral and mostly assumed; the central concern is the question of whether or not the Bennet sisters can each individually relate rightly to the right man. In *A Summer Bird-Cage* the relationship of the two sisters to the different men (plural in each case) in their separate lives is peripheral and assumed. . . . The central concern . . . is the question of what kind of a relationship will be established between the sisters, which represents a significant reordering of traditional priorities.[10]

As sisters become "central," the treatment of their communication grows more explicit. Clothes in particular constitute the vocabulary for complex negotiations involving identity. Other items, such as fireworks exploding during a quarrel, function as obvious symbols, drawing attention to the restrictions and artifice of the traditional plot.

These novels ultimately reshape convention, establishing a stance toward other women writers as well as patriarchal codes governing female behavior. Joanne Creighton's observation that Margaret Drabble's "mediating and often equivocal position between the traditional and the modern . . . makes her an important voice in contemporary fiction"[11] applies to Elizabeth Jane Howard and Barbara Pym as well. Their novels depict women who must deal with their interdependence. Many of the heroines live vicariously through their sisters; as they observe and comment on their siblings' lives, these women function as authorial surrogates within the narrative.

Barbara Pym inserts herself and her sister Hilary into *Some Tame Gazelle* and *An Unsuitable Attachment*, the earliest and latest to be published of the novels discussed in this chapter. Nevertheless, the world has changed little from one novel to the other; most of the women in *An Unsuitable Attachment* are employed, but they have little sense of vocation and continue to occupy themselves with parish affairs, gossip, and courtship. The sisters in both texts exist in apparent harmony, although one sister's penchant for living through her sibling ultimately creates difficulties.

On the surface, *Some Tame Gazelle* appears to be a conscious revision of *Cranford*, with its spinster sisters and active community of women. A fundamental difference exists, however. No patriarchal law hovers over the lives of Pym's characters as it does in Cranford. The men verge on being ridiculous: Archdeacon Henry Hoccleve is pedantic; Count Bianco is foolish; and the young curate, Mr. Donne, is immature. Because the men are ineffectual, the women have no need to ally themselves with them, as Deborah Jenkyns relies on the rector of Cranford's authority. Instead, Pym's heroines, Belinda and Harriet Bede, are virtually equal at home. Belinda manages practical matters and worries incessantly about etiquette, while Harriet plays the aging coquette.

The division of roles between the sisters is the traditional opposition. Robert Long describes it as a "caricature. . . . Harriet is plump and elegant, while Belinda is thin and almost dowdy. . . ." And Frederick Keener considers "Belinda's buxom sister Harriet—Sensibility in proportion to Belinda's Sense. . . ."[12] More specifically, Harriet worries about ordering fashionable clothes and criticizes the frumpy Belinda for hiding herself in old, shapeless garments or fussing about the seamstress's predilections. While Harriet flirts in flowered dresses, Belinda considers herself below the notice of men, asexual. Harriet thrives on homage and admiration; Belinda's solace is in solicitude.

In relationships with men, each woman has her territory. Harriet enjoys not only the quasi-filial respect of her curates but also the ritual of rejecting Count Bianco's proposals, while Belinda lives wistfully for Henry Hoccleve, a college friend who married another woman. The sisters exist in a constant state of titillation created by ungratified, postponed desire. Their first dinner with Mr. Donne is seasoned with "social niceties and sexual innuendo."[13] Belinda speculates about the curate's underwear; then Harriet offers him a ripe pear: "He seemed to be getting rather sticky and there was some giggling and interchange of large handkerchiefs between him and Harriet."[14] No physical contact occurs, but the sexually suggestive offer of fruit and the exchange of handkerchiefs provoke Harriet to "giggles" and "tittering" (17).

Because the sisters make no attempt to consummate heterosexual relationships, they need never confront the illusory nature of their hopes. Rarely do they feel disappointment; each curate, like each conversation with Henry, brings the possibility of success. This state of constant expectation is in many ways preferable to the staleness of such marriages as Henry Hoccleve's: "For Harriet curates are a renewable resource and so her relationships with them have a passion, a freshness, a timelessness that no marriage could supply."[15] In the end, unrequited love benefits both sisters. Harriet derives gratification from being sought, but not possessed, by the count. And life mending a curate's socks would be considerably less exciting than her world of possibilities. Belinda gains satisfaction from looking after others as well as from Henry's odd moments of appreciation, as when he invites her to tea.

Since the desired men, Henry and the curates, are equally unattainable, the siblings find little reason to compete with one another. Instead, each offers her sister what that sister seeks in a man. Harriet is often a little bossy (even though she is the youngest, she "behaves like an older sister," 99). She overlooks Belinda's abilities, just as Henry deprecates Belinda. Belinda allows Harriet to sort through her clothes and order her about in the same way as Harriet mothers her curates.

As in *Cranford*, the appearance of male outsiders unsettles the sisters' household. Yet Pym differs from Gaskell in offering her protagonists opportunities to marry. Mr. Mold, a librarian, and Theo Grote, an ex-suitor of Harriet's, are refused by Harriet and Belinda, respectively. The Bedes share Elizabeth Bennet's conviction in Austen's *Pride and Prejudice* that marriage for its own sake is an unacceptable alternative: "If merely being married or being loved were the point, Harriet would certainly marry her ardent Italian. . . ."[16] Moreover, the proposals indicate that the women do not indulge in unrequited love "because there is no one else" or "for lack of more suitable choices. . . ."[17] They are responsible for their position as spinsters, and not victims of society, circumstance, or economic necessity.

Not only are marriages averted, but proposals, or even the threat of them, are perceived as disruptions. Knowing that Harriet will refuse Count Bianco, Belinda can afford to show compassion toward him and tell him not to "lose hope" (213). Belinda also enjoys catering to Harriet's curates and gains vicarious pleasure in her sister's attractiveness to men, as long as she senses no real danger to her orderly existence: "Her only serious anxiety in the course of the novel is that the unpredictable Harriet might choose to marry Mr. Mold or Theo Grote."[18] Indeed, during Mr. Mold's visit, we are told:

> Had she [Belinda] known what was going on, she would probably have rushed into the drawing room, even if she had still been wearing her old gardening mackintosh and galoshes, and tried her best to stop it, for one was never quite sure what Harriet would do. (140)

On learning of her reprieve, "the look of relief that brightened Belinda's face was pathetic in its intensity" (142).

Diana Benet asserts that Belinda fears the proposals because they "represent the evils of change. . . ."[19] More than that, marriage involves a serious loss for each sister, depriving her of the qualities split off in her sibling and of the complementarity both have depended on for comfort and survival. Finally, marriage might precipitate a loss of illusions. Single, the Bedes have their affection for each other and their unrequited lovers; married, they might have neither. Expelled from the "world of romance, aspiration, love-longing, loneliness, despair," the women would be left only with the "extreme triviality"[20] of village life. Thus, in choosing singleness, the sisters retain the "sanctuaries of their imaginations. . . ."[21]

In leaving the sisters single by choice, Pym implicitly comments on convention. In contrast to the Misses Jenkyns in Gaskell's *Cranford*, the Bedes have suitors; unlike Charlotte Lucas in Austen's *Pride and Prejudice*, they have the financial resources to reject tiresome men; and in opposition to Miss Bates in Austen's *Emma*, they can remain spinsters without becoming caricatures. The apparent similarities to a "Victorian courtship novel"[22] are deceptive; "the romantic materials" are "dislocate[d]"[23] to create questions and discomfort in the minds of readers.

Specifically, while *Some Tame Gazelle* "celebrate[s] . . . singleness,"[24] it leaves several issues unresolved. First, because the sisters' singleness depends on indirect communication, innuendo, and illusion, their happiness is fragile. They are vulnerable in a world where an Agatha Hoccleve may propose directly to her beloved. Moreover, the sisters are isolated from other women. Although they have tea with Edith Liversedge and Connie Aspinall, they do not share the intimacy of Cranford's Amazons. Belinda finds Edith Liversedge "dishevelled," "brusque," and an "embarrassment" (29), and her distaste for Agatha Hoccleve is scarcely concealed when they quarrel over such petty matters as marrow squash. Harriet has fewer dealings with other women and views Belinda's defensive maneuvers with Miss Prior, the seamstress, with mixed impatience and disgust. She reserves her jealousy for Miss Berridge, Mr. Donne's intended, whom she considers "toothy" (235). The Bedes view their peers with envy, distrust, and anxiety, because other women can break up their dreams or force them to confront reality. This hostility appears discrepant in a novel that otherwise seems to celebrate female closeness; however, it is at the heart of Pym's intent as she depicts the complexity of relations among women.

Defensiveness can be found in other areas of the sisters' lives, too. Their relationship is not perfectly balanced, and they have spats over lunch menus and Belinda's apparel. As in more traditional sister novels, the women are preoccupied not only with satisfying their individual needs, but also with establishing mastery, even in the small circle of home. The difference is in frequency; the Bedes quarrel less often than some of their literary precursors.

Still greater defensiveness exists with regard to men and marriage, even though Pym presents the Bedes' singleness as a triumphant choice. The continuing antagonism and competition between Belinda and Agatha, as well as Harriet's envy of Mr. Donne's wife, imply incomplete acceptance of the situation. Belinda's pathetic observation of and incessant curiosity about the Hoccleve household underline this point. Her interest, down to knowing precisely what Agatha serves the seamstress for lunch, is purely critical, for she wishes to vindicate her sense of inferiority at not being chosen by Henry. The repression in the sisters' lives is apparent not only in the evening with Mr. Donne, but also in a meeting of women, which Janice Rossen calls an "impromptu frolic":

> This scenario reflects the blessings of the single state, but the characters' schoolgirlish behaviour strikes a slightly ironic note; it suggests a sort of immaturity. . . . Spinsterhood can reflect arrested development. . . ."[25]

Although the women have chosen to be single, they make no real accommodation to and have little contact with the larger world, where many do marry, make friends, and find sexual fulfillment. The imaginative life of the Bedes remains a defensive posture. Even as Pym pretends to glorify the choice of spinsterhood as part of her ironic comment on *Cranford,* she is bound to *Cranford*'s circumstance: the single sisters inhabit a realm of romance threatened by a world that reaches as far as London and Africa.

Indeed, to comment, as Rhonda Sherwood does, that "Pym's novel is a pleasure to read not just because it is an amusing spoof of romantic comedy but because its positive depiction of the Bede sisters acts as a corrective to the treatment given sisterhood"[26] in other novels is to ignore the darker side of Pym's text. Sherwood's denial of tension between the Bede sisters is an example of the way feminists respond to twentieth-century sister stories. Longings for closeness and harmony among women underlie Sherwood's remark as she glides from sisters to sisterhood, for, as I have shown, the Bedes themselves show little sisterhood toward other women. But more importantly, in considering Pym's story a "corrective," Sherwood suggests that negative depictions of sisters are somehow wrong or astray, and that there is a "correct" and proper way to (re)present sisterly relations.

The implications of this attitude are highly significant. First, in rejecting certain female behaviors, Sherwood herself participates in the ritual of role splitting with its accompanying denial of female anger. Like Elizabeth Gaskell before her, she inserts herself in another's story, playing the role of monitory older sibling, censuring and censoring unacceptable behavior. Her rejection of friction and enmity among sisters is less subtle than Gaskell's suppression of Charlotte Brontë's anger, although she, too, must manipulate dates. Whereas Gaskell must antedate Branwell Brontë's disastrous exploits, Sherwood ignores the fact that Pym's book was written before two of the novels it supposedly "corrects," works by Gail Godwin and Margaret Drabble.

In the end, Sherwood's efforts, which surpass Gaskell's attempts to create a sisterhood, resemble Nina Auerbach's idealization of Gaskell's women characters. While both Gaskell and Sherwood try to force characters into a mold of conventionally acceptable harmonious female behavior, Sherwood also denies friction in Pym's work because it is not politically "correct"—that is, she negates emotions that are at odds with an imperative for harmony and sisterhood. In doing so, she cuts out a crucial aspect of the sister story, excising part of its plot.

Pym herself alters the sister story, but without such radical surgery. In a later novel, *An Unsuitable Attachment*, she presents a different set of sisters. The Bedes appear only briefly in *An Unsuitable Attachment;* having inherited Count Bianco's wealth, they are being shepherded about Rome by a young curate, Basil Branche. The Bedes are marginal in the plot, serving primarily to explain Branche's appearance and to remind us of Pym's earlier view of sisterly relations. In addition, the Bedes are a deliberate contrast to two more worldly siblings, Penelope

Grandison and Sophia Ainger. The latter are more traditional novel heroines, being young and attractive. Thus, by using characters from an earlier book (as she often does), Pym draws attention to literary conventions as well as to herself and the work's intertextuality.

An Unsuitable Attachment takes place in a small London parish, where the vicar, Mark Ainger, makes the rounds of the West Indian neighborhoods. Most of the women in the novel work or have worked: Penelope has an office job, Ianthe Broome is employed in a library, Daisy Pettigrew assists in a veterinary clinic, and Sister Dew is a retired nurse. Only the married woman, Sophia Ainger, lacks an occupation.

Although the setting and circumstances in this novel are more contemporary than in *Some Tame Gazelle*, many of the same issues persist. The female characters have little sense of vocation, and employment outside the home does not significantly alter their lives. Penelope's occupation remains obscure; it is merely something that fills the hours and pays the bills. Ianthe chooses to work in a library because it is "necessary for her to do some kind of work" and her mother considers it "a ladylike occupation."[27] With men, the women are curiously conservative, as when Ianthe expects to be given a seat on the Underground. Similarly, Penelope intends to be walked home after dinner, and "like so many modern young women she had the right old-fashioned ideas about men and their work" (69).

Not surprisingly, then, little has changed between sisters. Sophia, the elder of the two, lavishes her affection on the cat, Faustina. Concerned with parish affairs and propriety, she resembles Celia Brooke Chettam in Eliot's *Middlemarch*, and her interests verge on obsessions. She has little else to occupy her, having neither job nor children, and frequently finding her husband cold and distant. Penelope is more dramatic, both in her personality and in her appearance:

> Penelope had the same colouring [as Sophia] and generally romantic air, but was shorter and dumpier with rather fat legs. She wore a black sacklike dress, a large silver medallion on a chain, black nylon stockings and flat-heeled shoes. Her hair was dressed in a 'beehive' style, which was now collapsing on one side. The Pre-Raphaelite beatnik. . . . (39)

Penelope's odd clothing reflects her insecurities; her flashy chain and high perched hair indicate a desire to be noticed, while her shapeless, colorless garments betray a lack of confidence in herself and her body. Moreover, the "collapsing" hair implies that Penelope has difficulty maintaining any polish she might wish to project. Penelope's appearance is in part a reaction against her sister, her trendy clothing and messy hair opposed to Sophia's conservative, neat apparel. Denying her sexuality with her baggy garments, she avoids an unhappy marriage like Sophia's.

Sophia's marriage has ostensibly eliminated competition for men; nevertheless, friction remains, however submerged. Sophia's unsatisfying relationship with her husband does not prevent her from contriving to introduce Penelope to Rupert Stonebird, a new neighbor: "Sophia was taking a keen interest in him and had even been considering him . . . as a husband for her sister" (35). Certainly, Sophia wishes her sibling to have companionship, but her "interest" is more self-serving and contradictory than that. No doubt Sophia perceives her sister's single state as a critical comment on her own marriage. At the same time, she takes vicarious pleasure in Penelope's exploits. If Penelope marries, Sophia will lose this source of excitement in her life; should Penelope's marriage be happier than hers, she might lose the gratification of looking after her sister, inviting her to dinner, and lending her suitable clothing. Penelope, in turn, senses her sister's ambivalent impulses.

The sisters unite, however, in Penelope's competition with Ianthe Broome, another neighbor, who initially succeeds in attracting Rupert Stonebird. Because she is an outside rival, Ianthe plays a role analogous to Mary Crawford's in Austen's *Mansfield Park*, although the women's personalities are almost contraries. Ianthe's taste and manners are impeccable. She wears old-fashioned classics—furs, silks, wools. None of her clothes are made of synthetic materials. Instead of being garish, Ianthe's garments tend to be faded. When Penelope remarks that Ianthe's scarf is "so tiresomely *good*, like all Ianthe's things" (123), her "good" seems morally loaded as well as a reference to the scarf's quality. Moreover, as Margaret Ezell notes, Ianthe is also a threat to the older sister, "being a canon's daughter who seems to be able to manage any parish or social affair with competent grace. Sophia . . . sees in Ianthe an elegant gentility she lost by marrying a poor clergyman."[28]

The tensions between the biological sisters and their neighbor "sister" are most apparent when Rupert invites Ianthe and others to a dinner party. The wife of one of his guests becomes ill at the last moment, so he asks Penelope. Penelope, lacking the time to change at home after work, stops at her sister's house to borrow party clothes. A muted struggle over apparel becomes an expression of the sisters' competing personalities.

The scene in which the two siblings pick a garment for Penelope is a comic vignette. Traditional Sophia may be eager to see Penelope married, but her budget is limited, and she worries that her harum-scarum sister might ruin one of her few good dresses: " 'There's my new green wool,' said Sophia, a little reluctantly, 'but I haven't worn it yet' " (121). The fear that her younger sister might wear the new dress first is powerful because Sophia is concerned that the dress will somehow be "broken in" by her sister, that it will become part of Penelope rather than of Sophia. In fact, Penelope does not properly appreciate the offer. To her, wool is too conventional, so she rejects the dress. Despite her misgivings, Sophia reiterates that the party outfit must be "suitable," and she tempts Penelope by saying that Ianthe will no doubt wear wool. This, of course, spurs Penelope to wear a different fabric, and, after the women reject yet another dress, Sophia remembers a parcel of hand-me-downs from a wealthy woman. Sophia thought they were "much too grand for me to wear. I am sure we could find something for you" (121).

Implicit in this discussion is the notion that what suits one sister's image is not appropriate to the other's. It is a version of Jane and Elizabeth Bennet's conversation in which each appears to be praising the other but is in fact asserting her own individuality. Here, a physical fit is the last factor considered. Penelope's rejections include subtle put-downs of Sophia's life, but the solution—someone else's cast-offs—neutralizes the loan somewhat. The clothes still come from Sophia, but they are more appropriate to Penelope's tastes:

> Half an hour later Pen was encased—for it was a fraction too tight for her—in the lamé cocktail dress with the hem roughly tacked up, the sequin trimming torn away from the neck and a string of black beads hanging below the waist. (122)

Predictably, Sophia offers a touch of good taste, a string of pearls, but "the beads seemed to go with the piled up hair style and long pointed-toe shoes that Penelope was wearing" (122).

One imagines that Penelope looks ridiculous, tottering in high heels and a narrow skirt. Yet, if her goal is to look different from Ianthe, she succeeds. After greeting her, Rupert notices:

> He was talking rather too much . . . but her appearance in the dress of silver lamé—like some kind of armour remembered from childhood play-acting . . .—was quite startling and such a contrast to Ianthe's sober blue dress (123).

The comparison of the dress to armor is appropriate, because for Penelope the party is battle; her quest is for a husband rather than a fair maiden. At the same time, "play-acting" in borrowed clothes,

Penelope appears childish (in contrast, on another occasion Rupert realizes that Ianthe's "silk dress and jacket brought back to him reveries of his mother at parish garden parties of his childhood" [209]).

Throughout the evening, Penelope feels awkward and uncomfortable, especially when comparing herself to the graceful Ianthe, who seems at ease in this gathering of anthropologists. When the women guests retire, they notice that Penelope has split the back of her dress. The debate that follows echoes the scene between sisters, but this time the guests are offering suggestions to a "despairing" (129) Penelope. Penelope rejects their assistance; she is upset at being exposed (literally and figuratively) before these other women, especially because one of them is her rival for a man's affections. Humiliation before the men occurs later, when she returns to the sitting room and must contrive to keep her back turned.

Penelope's "armour" has slipped despite her careful preparations. Ironically, such exposure is only an extreme version of what the sisters desired, for on some level, they must have been aware of the possibility of exposure when they selected such a tight dress. They wished for Penelope to be seen as a sexual object, to be noticed above Ianthe— but not so overtly. The language of clothes is intended to be subtle; their function is to communicate and draw attention by covering, not by exposing. Thus, the outfit succeeds almost too well, but even near success is failure. Discovering the tear, Rupert finds Pen "provocative and rather endearing" (131). He is about to kiss her, but Sophia reappears, and Penelope enters "the house with head bent, feeling that she had been a failure" (131), ignorant of the unfortunate effects of her sister's interference.

Penelope's disastrous choice of dress is influenced by her wish to be different from her sister as well as from Ianthe. What the dress reveals in its tightness and gaudiness is her ambivalence as well as her sister's contradictory impulses. Sophia, by instigating the loan and reappearing at the wrong moment, shows herself helpful and harmful throughout, and, ultimately, both women are exposed.

Trading clothing in an attempt to alter her sister's image is no more effective or satisfying for Sophia than her efforts to live through Penelope. In fact, Penelope finally attracts Rupert's attention not because Sophia has fulfilled her "duty to her sister" (193) but because Ianthe marries another man. In a displacement of the traditional sister story, Ianthe chooses John Challow, who "could be . . . well, a younger brother" (96). Rupert, who has played the role of the paternal comforter, is free to marry Penelope. As in earlier novels, such as *Emma* and *Mansfield Park*, competition from an outside rival and the near loss of the suitor lead a character to marry. The only difference is that the "perfect" rival gains the brotherly lover, and the young sister wins the fatherly man.

Significantly, Sophia is disturbed by Ianthe's marriage, wishing her neighbor had remained single: "I never thought of her as getting married—it seems all wrong . . ." (247). Sophia's dismay seems out of proportion to the occasion; after all, Ianthe is little more than an acquaintance. However, Sophia's disappointment is comprehensible when one considers Diana Benet's assertion that "these people are unconsciously creative as they watch each other. . . ."[29] Much of Sophia's pleasure, like that of the Bede sisters, has come from the imagination, and she "wanted her [Ianthe] to stay as she was, almost as if . . . [she had] created her" (247). Ianthe, with her flawless clothes and manners, has played a crucial part in Sophia's schemes, keeping them at an exhilarating pitch where success remains just beyond reach. By removing herself as an obstacle to Penelope's marriage, Ianthe threatens Sophia's excitement. She challenges Sophia's confidence as she enters a marriage that may well be happier than her neighbor's. Most of all, Ianthe has served as a focus of displaced emotions for Sophia. As a block in Penelope's life, she has often acted out Sophia's hidden impulses; her utter propriety is merely an extreme version of Sophia's conservatism. Faced with Ianthe's marriage, Sophia feels abandoned. Ianthe is not what Sophia imagined—instead of being an extension of Sophia's will, she is a separate individual. In her anger, Sophia projects on Ianthe all the rivalry and hostility she cannot express toward her sister.

In *An Unsuitable Attachment*, then, Pym presents the problem of a sister who lives vicariously through her sibling. The unexpected marriage of an unrelated "sister" forces the characters to reassess their stances toward convention as well as their self-images. Sisterhood outside the family is not possible, because a friend becomes the repository of repressed emotions. Harmony between siblings is a frail and temporary illusion, bought at the expense of friendship with other women; the ideal of sisterhood must be relinquished when hostile feelings are projected onto an unrelated woman. Thus, Pym's novels respond pointedly to Gaskell, whose vision of sisterhood is achieved when biological siblings are distanced from each other: in *Cranford* one sister dies, in *Wives and Daughters* a sister is turned into a friend, and in *The Life of Charlotte Brontë*, Brontë is detached from her biological sisters, allowing her to become Gaskell's friend and sister. Moreover, her depictions of the friction among unrelated women suggest that twentieth-century critics' glorification of sisterhood is a cozy illusion at best, and a dangerous illusion at worst.

In Elizabeth Jane Howard's *After Julius*, similar issues surface in a triangle of women consisting of two sisters, Emma and Cressida, and their widowed mother. As in *An Unsuitable Attachment*, an expression of the sisters' relationship toward each other is found when they trade clothes; in *After Julius*, however, they swap roles with apparel, and Howard's attempted solution to the problem of sisters' individuation lies in this reversal.

As in other sister stories, Cressida and Emma are presented as opposing personalities. Cressida is beautiful, even more promiscuous than her namesake, and troubled. Lackadaisical about her career as a pianist, she has a self-destructive penchant for affairs with married men. She rarely returns to her childhood home, and, when she does, she entertains herself by arguing with her mother. In conventional terms, she is a "bad" girl, whereas her sister Emma is "good." Emma is timid and sexually inexperienced; at times she appears childish, as in her frequent weekend visits to her mother. Despite the fact that she holds a responsible position in her father's publishing firm, she does not take her career seriously, having chosen it after she "failed to do anything which she privately thought worthwhile . . ." (16). The sisters live together fairly harmoniously. While Emma picks up after Cressida, literally and figuratively, Cressida makes enough amorous mistakes for two. Acting as a monitory exemplar, she enables Emma to retain romantic illusions for herself.

The equilibrium is disrupted as the book opens, however. Intrigued by the peculiarities of one of her authors, Emma invites him home for the weekend. Esme, the girls' mother, is expecting a visitor, too, her ex-lover Felix. The appearance of these two men, one a stranger and the other absent for twenty years, unsettles the lives of the three women. The author, Dan, puzzles both sisters but charms Emma with his simplicity and childlike delight in sweets. Failing to recognize him as a suitor, Emma perceives Dan as a "brother" (140). Therefore, like her literary predecessors, Molly Gibson and Fanny Price, she initially finds her suitor less threatening than other men. He in turn is piqued by Emma's sympathy and understanding, even though he instinctively distrusts women. He is awed by Cressida's beauty and critical of her behavior, considering her "a tart" (132). Worse, "he was afraid that Emma might turn out to be like her sister . . ." (104). Aware of Dan's opinion of Cressida, Emma defends her sister nonetheless. The two women have not developed separate identities; consequently, when Dan criticizes Cressida, Emma, too, feels condemned. In fact, Cressida, like Sophia in *An Unsuitable Attachment*, plays a mixed part in her sister's romance; she may contrive to help, but her way of life is unacceptable to Dan. She unwittingly confirms Dan's suspicions about her when Esme's Saturday dinner guests include Cressida's lover and his wife.

In a scene that parallels Sophia and Penelope selecting clothes, Emma seeks Cressida's assistance in dressing for dinner. In this episode, her connectedness to Cressida is apparent when she reveals that she wishes to radiate some of her sibling's sexuality. Although Dan is the first male to attract Emma in years, Cressida has resolved to reform herself and to renounce men. The sisters thus reverse roles. As Cressida casts off her lover, so she casts off her apparel: "a tremendous clearing out of clothes in her room—a lot of them were not going to be suitable for her new life, and others she was simply tired of . . ." (135). Hoping to be unobtrusive, Cressida wears black. Emma adopts some of Cressida's rejected garments, selecting a revealing sleeveless cashmere sweater, cinched tightly at the waist with a belt.

The evening is an unmitigated disaster. Jennifer Hammond, the wife of Cressida's lover, discovers the affair before Cressida can terminate it. Jennifer confronts Cressy cruelly, and Emma comes to her sister's defense, begging the Hammonds to leave. Sickened by the scene, Dan decides to depart, too. In this way, the "helpful," experienced, older sister ruins her sibling's evening; her affair unleashes a chain of events, including Jennifer Hammond's discovery and Dan's betrayal, which ultimately leave Emma hurt and alone.

This scene, however, is not the end of the novel, for the reversal continues. Felix returns to London with Cressida. Refusing to make love to her, he claims that she has allowed herself to be emotionally violated by too many men. He will wait for her affection, and he orders her not to undress. Dan, on the other hand, returns with Emma to the girls' London flat. Seeing her in a revealing wrap bathrobe (significantly, one selected by Cressy), he imagines that Emma, too, is sexually experienced. Emma, "like a petrified doll" (248), allows herself to be raped. Only afterward does Dan realize what has occurred, as Emma is lying "broken" (250).

In *After Julius*, neither woman can achieve happiness until she has traveled her sister's path. Cressida must be with a man without having sex; Emma is raped. At various points in the reversal, each woman is seen as a prostitute or "tart." Not only does the woman who borrows become a powerless "doll," but, by taking another's image, she sells herself.

As the sisters reverse positions, they attempt to come to terms with patriarchal standards of behavior they have internalized as well as with each other. For Cressida, being a "bad girl" is unsatisfying; as a "good girl," Emma, like Molly Gibson, finds herself isolated. The rules governing women's conduct are simply inadequate, a point implicit in the book's title (Julius is the girls' father): Howard's novel is "after" the father's in being imitative of the courtship plot, but it is also "after" the father's in seeking a story to replace it. Finally, it is "after" the father in its attack on his standards.

The father's story, sent to Esme by his brother, is embedded in the text. A protracted account of events occurring twenty years before those in the novel, it initially appears redundant and digressive. But Julius's death has determined the other characters' behavior. His manuscript implies that he sacrificed himself after becoming aware of Esme's infidelity, and that his death was no passive acknowledgment of impotence or failure. It was a tremendous power play; he died a war hero, a martyr, a scapegoat to a woman's loose faith. Afterward, guilt separated Esme and Felix. Cressida's knowledge of the events contributed to her cynicism concerning sex, and the lack of a paternal model left Emma uneasy in the presence of men.

Occurrences in the novel alter the situation. Discovering that they have little in common, Felix and Esme can no longer blame Julius for making them feel inadequate and driving them apart. Felix, who has drifted most of his adult life, makes an active choice to pursue Cressida; in doing so, he replaces the father he and Esme deprived her of as a teenager. Finding a lover who is a poet like her father, Emma allows romance to enter her life.

The conclusion of Howard's novel is not entirely satisfying, however. Esme retires to her room to read *Pride and Prejudice;* thus, the mother, representing the female past and its literary traditions, remains alone and rejected. In addition, although the sisters' closeness persists, they continue to be isolated from other women. Neither expresses sympathy for Jennifer Hammond. The author hints, too, that Emma's relationship with the poetic Dan may eventually be a repetition of her parents' marriage, which failed because "poetry was his [Julius's] prevailing passion," and "in all moments of emotion he resorted to poetry . . ." (22). In the end, then, Howard hedges on the possibility of change; the stale words of male poets linger in a conclusion that echoes the appearance of Johnson's collected works at the end of *Cranford*.

Howard also emphasizes the persistence of tradition in her use of stock images and obvious symbols. Specifically, the fireworks after the explosive dinner and the parallel between Cressida's and Esme's promiscuity draw attention to the construction of the novel. Often, symbolism is so apparent as to seem aesthetically naïve, as when Emma indulges in a ritualistic bath before making love with Dan. Such obvious techniques reveal the conventional aspects of the sisters' story, as well as the inherent emptiness of its divisions and signs. Thus, even as Howard questions the possibility of change, she stresses the need to strive for a new text, a story "after" the father's.

In her first novel, *A Summer Bird-Cage*, Margaret Drabble, too, attempts to refashion the patriarchal sister story; like Howard, she manipulates imagery to draw attention to its inadequacy. Ultimately, the rift between sign and referent is related to a split between the concept of sisterhood and actual sisterly behavior, a division that was apparent in Gaskell's and Eliot's portrayals of sisters.

The intense focus on sisters in *A Summer Bird-Cage* suggests that Drabble herself is attempting to resolve questions about the nature of sisterhood in her own life. Her description of a growing rift between herself and her eldest sibling, A. S. Byatt, who herself has written several novels on sisters, parallels a passage in *A Summer Bird-Cage*. Of herself and Byatt, Drabble says:

> I used to tag along after her and she was always . . . well, she used to play with me a lot when we were little . . . I think this is what went wrong. I used to expect her to go on playing with me and of course she got bigger and didn't want me around. That made me sad and I always felt that I had been shut out, rejected by her.[30]

The heroine of *A Summer Bird-Cage*, Sarah Bennett, echoes her creator:

> I remember the ends of term, when she would come home from boarding school . . . I would cross the days off on my calendar for the last fortnight of term with excitement. . . . And every time she came there would be the same cold disillusion, the same sharp lesson in withdrawal. (101–102)

Sarah must resolve her continuing attraction to and irritation with her sister; her conflicting emotions reflect Drabble's experience. In fact, in an interview, Margaret Drabble referred to the first person narration in the novel as an "impersonation": "The narrator, who I suppose is me," addresses readers in a voice that is "close to the speaking vocabulary that I had at that age."[31]

Just as *A Summer Bird-Cage* involves a complicated series of communications between Sarah and her sibling, so the novel, together with Drabble's later works, constitutes part of an extended conversation with the writer's own sister. Byatt's fictions, especially *The Game* and *Still Life*, portray sisters struggling to assert their own identities. In *The Game*, for instance, one woman appropriates and destroys her sibling's life by writing a novel exposing her sister's secrets.[32] As Joanne Creighton has indicated, the characters in both women's books constantly create and recreate their sisters' lives, suggesting "that a certain amount of 'monstrous' appropriation of others is essential for the artist, including the female artist who has been taught that such aggression is 'unfeminine.' "[33] In both novels mentioned above, Byatt resolves sisterly conflicts conventionally, using the death of one sister to create distance as Gaskell does in *Cranford*. In contrast, Drabble's characters achieve a fuller understanding of their interdependence and ultimately come to terms with their differences.

In addition to drawing on biographical details, Drabble sets her heroines against portraits of sisters in earlier literature and has them respond to these nonbiological siblings. Drabble's comments on pre-texts are more intricate and revealing than those of Pym and Howard, illustrating the effects of characters' misreadings—as well as readings—of earlier novels. As I have indicated, an obvious precursor to the novel is *Pride and Prejudice*, a work about another set of Bennet(t) sisters. As Arnold Davidson asserts, Sarah, like Elizabeth Bennet, must come to terms with her pride and prejudice. He compares Louise to Jane Bennet "in that she weds a man who is socially most suitable" and to Lydia in her "openly licentious behavior."[34]

Margaret Drabble has acknowledged basing the plot of *A Summer Bird-Cage* on *Middlemarch*[35] as well as on *Pride and Prejudice*, and Susanna Roxman has traced similarities between Drabble's Louise and Eliot's Dorothea Brooke: "They are both dark and exceptionally beautiful; they are moreover intelligent, intense, and serious. Their sisters are a little afraid of them. . . . Sarah and Celia have fewer traits in common."[36] The similarities are more ironic than not; Louise's frequently cold, cruel, and mercenary behavior contradicts Dorothea's warm, compassionate, and unselfish actions.

Drabble's most radical use of pre-texts occurs within the story as characters misinterpret other novels. During a rare evening of friendship between the Bennett sisters, Sarah is "struck as we sat there by the charming convention of the scene—sisters idling away an odd evening in happy companionship. It was like something out of *Middlemarch* or even Jane Austen" (171). Sarah's "charming convention" is, in fact, anything but harmony and light. Dorothea would sniff at the very idea of "idling" an evening, and her conversation with Celia is frequently full of barbs. Sisters in Austen, too, are likely to be spiteful.

Nevertheless, Sarah persists in her conviction that the hostility between her and Louise is atypical. She insists that some sisters would immediately get together after one had returned from a trip to the Continent, and that others would invite each other to their parties, "but we didn't belong to either of these groups" (101). This sense of abnormality lends an air of defensiveness to Sarah's narrative as she strives to justify and rationalize her relationship with Louise.

Sarah's feeling of isolation is accentuated by her consciousness of not "belonging" to a tradition of sisters, and she experiences intense role confusion. When she considers the story of Cinderella, she does not know whether she is the heroine "or rather one of her ugly sisters" (14). Reluctant to place herself in a line of hostile siblings, Sarah is convinced that anger is "bad," and, like Molly Gibson in Gaskell's *Wives and Daughters*, she constantly suppresses it, denying even literary examples of friction among siblings. For instance, she does not select Gwendolen Harleth from Eliot's *Daniel Deronda* as a model. She strives to squelch emotions that do not conform to her ideals of feminine behavior. As Sarah pushes away undesirable emotions, Louise, stunningly beautiful like Cressida in *After Julius*, comes to represent all Sarah's "bad" impulses.

Louise is the "Snow Queen" (46), cold and distant toward her sister and others: "She was never a one for touching people . . ." (27). Occasionally, she makes brief appearances in Sarah's life, a prima donna collecting accolades. Dropping in on Sarah unannounced at Oxford, Louise takes her younger sibling out to lunch and shows off not one but two male escorts. Sarah is hurt by Louise's behavior and longs for the closeness she imagines literary sisters experience. This desire is revealed when Sarah finds herself "honoured" by a rare instant of "accessibility" (23) in Louise.

Sarah benefits, too, from her sister's icy elegance. Louise has a certain notoriety; one of Louise's friends takes Sarah out for the sole purpose of gossiping about Louise's scandalous affair. After Louise's marriage, Sarah is invited to luxurious dinner parties and admitted to the inner circle of London celebrities. If Louise enjoys being set off by her frumpier sister, Sarah gains a puritanical sense of superiority from her sister's disasters. Louise and her lover may have "needed an audience to build up the striking, wicked image of themselves," but Sarah profits, too, "gazing with admiration into the dangerous caves of the fiercer breed. I didn't mind. It soothed my conscience" (187). Like the Dashwoods in Austen's *Sense and Sensibility*, Drabble's sisters depend on each other's reactions, which are predictable and self-affirming.

What Sarah fails to acknowledge is that Louise's "vacant" (27) behavior is only an exaggeration of her own dislike of intimacy. Sarah's discomfort at buttoning up her sister's dress, "I could feel her hard breasts rising and falling under my clumsy hands" (27), signals a "subtle eroticism"[37] between the sisters. This "eroticism" is an extreme version of Cynthia Kirkpatrick's "seduction" of Molly Gibson in Gaskell's *Wives and Daughters*, which initiates the latter into the world of sisterly competition. Yet neither one of Drabble's sisters admits attraction or resemblance, and by emphasizing Louise's detachment and beauty in contrast to her own awkwardness, Sarah is able to maintain her distance. In fact, Sarah desires Louise's body in its audacious, sexual flaunting of patriarchal rules, but she also perceives it as dangerous and disruptive. Her mixed emotions echo Molly Gibson's views of Cynthia Kirkpatrick's dalliances with every man in sight. As Virginia Beards comments, "here is a woman who has internalized the values of her culture yet who, unfortunately, still wanly questions them."[38] Sarah fears incest and lesbianism, not only because they are taboo, but also because she believes they might involve merging her identity with Louise's. Her insistence on differences is a more dramatic version of Elizabeth Bennet's dismay at Lydia's flirtatious exhibition of her charms in Austen's *Pride and Prejudice*, which is also a display of her sexuality.

Yet, Sarah is different from Austen's sisters in that she does not accept sisterly secrecy. Whereas Marianne Dashwood and Elizabeth Elliott show little interest in the workings of their siblings' minds, Sarah is troubled by the enigmatic nature of Louise's distance: "I wondered why she was such a mystery. . . . And yet I suppose that I knew more facts about Louise than about anyone else in the world . . ." (67). Sarah considers Louise's opacity her own failure; "I felt my powers of deduction were at fault" (67), another sign that their relationship is aberrant. The little that Louise offers Sarah and the world is a performance. Her apartment has the air of a "film set" (130), perfectly matched and decorated. Sensing the artifice in her sister's life, Sarah explains how Louise might wear dirty underwear under her splendid silk wedding gown (27), for "she had never been tidy behind the scenes, as it were, but only for show" (120). Louise's inconsistencies frustrate Sarah, reminding her that she does not know what is "behind the scenes" or comprehend her sister's reasons for marrying.

Exploring her sister's bedroom, speculating with friends about Louise's intimate life, reading her diary—Sarah considers knowledge of Louise's most private moments her right, her territory. She is so "fascinated with the details of Louise's private life"[39] that her interest verges on obsession; Sarah even compares herself to a "voyeuse" (73).

Sarah's curiosity has two facets. First, it is competitive. Her study of every intricacy of Louise's appearance, culminating in the discovery that Louise's bright red lipstick is a "disastrous error" (118), is designed to make her feel superior to her seemingly flawless sister. Studying Louise, Sarah is studying the *other*, the rival, the woman who reminds her of her redundancy in the family, her "age-old, cradle-born superfluity" (21). At the same time, Sarah's conviction that Louise has no right to privacy implies that she recognizes no separation between herself and her sibling, that the *other* is in fact part of herself, only suppressed. In Joanne Creighton's astute assessment of the relationship,

> Sarah is obsessed with her older sister Louise, to whom she is bound in a competitive, uncommunicative, yet symbiotic relationship. Repulsed by Louise's coveting of material possessions and social smartness, Sarah, however, *understands neither Louise nor the part of herself which is like her sister.*[40]

When Louise gazes at herself in the mirror, it is as "though she were some object foreign to herself" (132); the same might be said of Sarah gazing in the mirror at herself or Louise.

Sarah's relationship with Louise is a model, albeit an extreme one, for her dealings with other women. On the surface, Sarah gets along better with her peers than with Louise. She shares an apartment with Gill, a newly separated woman, but their friendship rapidly deteriorates as Sarah replays her relationship with Louise. Sarah expects Gill to clean up after her, as if Gill were the seemingly impeccable Louise. When Gill is distressed about her marriage, Sarah distances herself, finding it "terrifying" (107) that this "sister" is not as resilient as her idol, Louise. With her dowdy cousin Daphne, Sarah is even less comfortable, for she sees in Daphne an exaggerated version of her own clumsiness. Sarah plays Louise's role of noblesse oblige, graciously inviting her cousin for tea with her and a male friend. Significantly, when Sarah learns that she has more in common with Louise than with Daphne, she ceases to feel any obligation to treat Daphne well. Thus, as Elizabeth Fox-Genovese asserts, Sarah and Louise (like other Drabble heroines) "defiantly live at the expense of other women."[41] Sarah blames her sister for her alienation from her peers:

> In the end she taught me the art of competition, and this is what I really hold against her: I think I had as little desire to outdo others in my nature as a person can have, until she insisted on demonstrating her superiority. She taught me to want to outdo her. (103)

Sarah takes no responsibility for her own acts, although she is as competitive as Louise. She has split off yet another aspect of herself, denied it, and assigned it to her sister.

The situation changes when Louise is caught by her husband while she is bathing with her lover. Pretensions to invulnerability are stripped with her clothing, and she turns to Sarah for help. This reversal—with the glamorous Louise arriving on Sarah's doorstep clad only in a bathrobe—initiates a reassessment of the "complementarity so profound that they are dependent on each other for identity."[42] Just before that, Louise had taken Sarah backstage at the theater; now she invites her sister backstage in her own life. As a result, Sarah, like Gwendolen Harleth in *Daniel Deronda* and Celia Brooke in *Middlemarch*, learns to accept her resemblance to her sister. Instead of being an "inverse double,"[43] Sarah, too, finds herself attractive, mercenary, lost: "Sympathy in Sarah's consciousness, leads to a self-recognition that also stresses . . . similarity. . . ."[44]

The knowledge that Louise is vulnerable and that she (Sarah) has the power to refuse Louise comfort releases Sarah from anger. Sarah, who initially confessed, "I hate being parted from my luggage" (10), admits at the end:

> Something very very old snapped in me. It snapped as though it had been a piece of old and rotten string, long useless, long without any power to tie, and yet still wrapped round and confining an ancient parcel of fears and prejudices. It snapped and the parcel spilled apart all over the floor. (191–92)

Rhonda Sherwood considers this string an allusion to the umbilical cord,[45] but, placed as it is in a narrative concentrating on sisters, the string is more likely to refer to Sarah's relations with Louise than to those with her mother. The tie, "very very old" and "long useless," is Sarah's outworn notion of sisterly behavior, and the "parcel of fears and prejudices" contains her emotions about living up to this notion. Or, to put it another way, the "tie" is Sarah's ideal of sisterhood, and the "parcel" is the actual set of emotions making up the relationship.

Unknotted at this time are all of Sarah's fictions, not only about sisterly behavior in general, but also about Louise. Just as the characters in *An Unsuitable Attachment* must acknowledge that their conception of Ianthe is a fiction, Sarah must realize that she has created the Louise she describes:

> She was merely and accidentally my sister whereas Simone [a friend] was a personal person of my own.
> This is a lie, but a lie that I am often near to believing. (72)

If it is a "lie" that Louise is "merely and accidentally" Sarah's sister, then Louise, too, is a "personal person" created by Sarah. Indeed, the created Louise is part of Sarah—her fear of intimacy, her suppressed eroticism, her competitiveness with other women—the part Sarah, like many critics, has struggled so hard to "correct." To believe that Louise is anything (or anyone) else is a "lie."

As the parcel of Sarah's metaphor slips apart, so does the metaphor of sisterhood, which is as illusory as any human creation. In the absence of intimacy between sisters, Sarah wishes her sister were "merely and accidentally" a biological relative, with no "personal" influence or effect. Sarah's almost puritanical criticism of Louise is a reflection of this desire for simplicity and "mere" connotation in the term *sister*. She longs for Louise to be as she "almost" is on her wedding day, "the real thing . . . meaningless and pure. . . . By virtue of form, not content. Symbol, not moral" (33).

In the course of the novel, Sarah finds that the desire to divide "symbol" from "moral" (or "form"—biological kinship—from "content"—metaphorical relationship) involves a deep and troubling split in herself. Yet if she cannot have what is "pure and meaningless," or its opposite, the "long useless" ideal of sisterhood, what remains?

Drabble may unpack the "parcel," but she offers no satisfying solution for Sarah, no easy unity:

> This impulse to seize on one moment as a whole, . . . one attitude as a revelation, is the impulse that . . . confounds and impels us. To force a unity from a quarrel, a high continuum from a sequence of defeats and petty disasters, to live on the level of the heart rather than the level of the slipping petticoat, this is what we spend our life on, and this is what wears us out. (206)

Louise and Sarah develop friendlier relations with each other, even share secrets, once they acknowledge their complementarity and similarity. Neither one must relinquish her personality, as Dorothea does when Celia asserts their commonalities in *Middlemarch*. However, the novel ends with the "slipping petticoat," curiously akin to Penelope Grandison's split dress in Pym's *Unsuitable Attachment*, and reminiscent of Louise's exposure in the tub. The "petticoat" fashioned of "petty disasters" is inevitably displayed or "worn out," even as it "confounds" or "wears out" its owner. Similarly, the "parcel" is never refastened, and no new seams are sewn. Drabble's answer, then, is limited and individual, based on the particular and literal rather than the "total" or "symbolic." She gives us an example of sisters who communicate, but no Amazonian girdle of sisterhood. As Elizabeth Fox-Genovese argues,

> Drabble so seduces with her illusion of referents, [that] she exposes herself to deep reproach for her failure to deliver: reproach, that is, for the

particular intellectual narcissism that plays with meaning, promises meaning, offers communication. . . .[46]

Like Elizabeth Jane Howard and Barbara Pym, Margaret Drabble sketches a story "after" the patriarchal code and nineteenth-century novels (both imitative and subsequent), but she offers no general solution. Her contribution to our understanding of sisterly relations lies in her meticulous exposition of the restrictive nature of definitions of sisterhood, both those inherited from patriarchal conventions and those apparent in recent feminist criticism. Her work is an expression in fiction of what Helena Michie, too, has noticed: that such terms as *sister* "become vessels that contain, shape, and delimit feminist discourse just as the family as it is now construed contains and shapes the roles and bodies of 'real' mothers and sisters."[47]

Ultimately, then, none of the authors discussed in this chapter offers an entirely satisfying conclusion. Readers may feel betrayed after they sympathize with such characters as Sarah who seek an end to female competition and hostility. However, these writers do not deserve "deep reproach" for not "delivering"; as Drabble has indicated, neatly tied "parcels" are no longer possible. Instead of closure, these authors seek openness, questioning the very ideal that classifies certain female behaviors as wrong or in need of correction. They imply that women who believe blindly in the ideal are overlooking a tradition of texts in which women do not get along. Moreover, to conform to such ideals, women must cut off and disown parts of themselves, just as Cinderella's stepsisters amputate their toes to fit her shoes. What is necessary is a new definition of sisterhood, one that is neither merely descriptive of a biological relationship nor prescriptive of female behavior. In demonstrating this need and in challenging traditional definitions, Drabble, Pym, and Howard are pressing for a mode of sisterhood "after" the father.

6

Conclusion

Killing the Good Sister; or, The Return of the Witch

Torn between a political desire for a harmonious sisterhood and the frustration of a tense relationship with her blood sister, Margaret Drabble's Sarah embodies the predicament of the contemporary heroine. Critics' frequent silences and discomfort surrounding the subject of biological sisters mask a similar disappointment in the disparity between ideal and actuality. Luise Eichenbaum and Susie Orbach have described this discomfort as "a post-feminist self-imposed censorship on certain feelings that women consider unacceptable. Feelings, for example, of competition and envy. . . ."[1]

The problem is a significant one for the women's movement as well as for novelists and literary critics. How does one learn to value difference and disagreement as well as common principles? The continuing debate over surrogate motherhood, which was precipitated by the "Baby M" case, has split feminists; women with clashing convictions claim their position to be the "true" feminist stand, condemning those who oppose them as being classist and racist as well as sexist. More recently, the furor surrounding the 1990 National Women's Studies Association convention exemplifies women's dilemma. A group of women disrupted the conference to protest the firing of a NWSA employee, claiming that her dismissal was evidence of racial discrimination within the organization. The hurt feelings and accusations of betrayal on both sides reflect women's difficulties in accepting discord within their ranks and their continuing belief that, among themselves, all must be harmonious.

Women obviously do not wish to portray themselves as disloyal or envious individuals just as they attain positions of respect and responsibility. Yet in valuing only the "good," pacifying emotions, they risk stifling a part of themselves. Coming to terms with a sister, be she a friend or a relative who embodies negative (or simply different) emotions, is therefore vital.

The importance of this issue is apparent in contemporary novels by

119

American and British women. Whereas in nineteenth-century works, the sister story is usually of secondary importance to the courtship convention, books published after *A Summer Bird-Cage* scrutinize sisters' relationships more and more closely. In fact, the sister plot sometimes *becomes* the marriage plot, when intimate relations among women and lesbian affairs replace heterosexual romance. Recent novels in English focusing on sisters include Marilynne Robinson's *Housekeeping*, Gail Godwin's *Mother and Two Daughters* as well as *Odd Woman*, Alice Walker's *Color Purple*, Ursula Holden's *Wider Pools*, Judith Rossner's *His Little Women*, Nancy Thayer's *Three Women at the Water's Edge*, and Emma Tennant's *Bad Sister*.[2] These books testify to the importance of biological sisters, but they also illustrate the necessity of coming to terms with other women as individuals—apart from the political imperative to feel sisterhood toward women collectively.

Although I have confined my study primarily to British texts, I wish to comment on several American novels that present more positive solutions to the problems of sisters than the works discussed in the last chapter. Toni Morrison's *Sula* traces the effects of distance on non-biological sisters who are eventually reunited.[3] Similarly, in *The Color Purple*, Alice Walker's heroine Celie and her sister are able to form distinct personalities during a prolonged separation. A relationship between Celie and Shug Avery replaces sisterly intimacy as well as heterosexual love; instead of trading sexually revealing dresses with her peers like Howard's and Pym's heroines, Celie tailors trousers, traditionally reserved for males, for the women in her life. Ultimately, then, these novels suggest a cruel irony, that the painful physical separations experienced in many Afro-American families may facilitate the development of female identity.

An element that is beginning to appear even more often is a stretching of the conventions of the realistic novel. The constricting nature of these forms is apparent in the obvious coincidences in Howard's and Drabble's works, and other novelists have begun simply to abandon the traditions. Their works hint at alternative ways of constructing or portraying female character, as well as at new modes of defining feminine experience.

In *The Color Purple*, for instance, Alice Walker applies an old convention, the epistolary form, to original materials. Her novel consists of letters written by a nearly illiterate woman to God and her sister Nettie. Celie's language undermines the rules of male grammar; at the same time, because her husband suppresses the letters, much of the novel is in fact a dialogue with the self.

Although Nettie has two existences, neither impinges on her sister. In Africa, Nettie engages in a complicated relationship with another

woman, Corrine, as they attempt to define their sisterhood. Corrine
and her husband, Samuel, are Nettie's employers, but when they all
move to Africa, the three become increasingly close. Corrine denies
feeling any jealousy, but she insists that Nettie call her and Samuel
sister and brother, claiming that the Africans might otherwise mistake
Nettie for Samuel's "other" wife.[4] Corrine's fear mirrors biological
sisters' consciousness of their redundancy, as well as their awareness of
the scarcity of love. In fact, after Corrine's death, Nettie does marry
Samuel; adopting her friend's surname, she takes on part of her
identity. Nettie's preoccupation with a nonbiological sister, together
with geographical distance, gives her little influence in Celie's life. In
her other existence as part of Celie's imagination, Nettie is equally
powerless, for she is easily controlled.

Instead of being trapped in a daily struggle with her sister, Celie is
free to participate in a sisterhood of "amazons,"[5] women brought
together by men and by frequently physical suffering rather than by
choice like *Cranford*'s Amazons. Celie initially meets Shug when the
latter is her husband's mistress. For both, homosexual intimacy gradually replaces heterosexual relations based on power and cruelty, as
Celie learns to express desire for an unrelated woman. She need not
break the incest taboo that makes Drabble's Sarah so uncomfortable
with Louise in *A Summer Bird-Cage*. Thus, even as Alice Walker
proceeds beyond the authors discussed in the last chapter to abandon
the fiction of character and the illusion that two sisters might be fully
separate, she reshapes romance.

Marilynne Robinson's *Housekeeping* traces the bonds of sisters
through several generations, recording family history in a uniquely
feminist and intricate mode. The heroine and her sister are raised by
their grandmother and, after her death, by their great-aunts. When
the latter prove unequal to the task, the girls' wandering Aunt Sylvie
reluctantly agrees to stay with them. Sylvie's return creates an initial
irony; although she has been considered the black sheep in the family,
she comes to care for the orphan girls, who have been abandoned by
the suicide of their more conventional mother (appropriately named
after Helen of Troy, another woman who deserted her family). Nurturing the orphans, she "reminds" the heroine, Ruth, of her mother,
until "Sylvie began to blur the memory . . . and then to displace it."[6]
Categories begin to dissolve; the "bad" aunt turns out to be more
caring than the "good" mother, and in the process distinctions between characters are abolished.

Sylvie is alien to the constricted society of Fingerbone, a town
whose very name suggests its dryness and lifelessness, as well as the
fingers townspeople point at those bold enough to revolt against their

conventions. Sylvie shows little tolerance for the town's suffocating atmosphere. Under her influence, the house, "a mere mound, no more a human stronghold than a grave,"[7] becomes open to wind and rain. Piles of empty cans and old newspapers clutter the rooms, detritus and history alike turned to decoration. Sylvie encourages the girls to break the town's rules for women, dressing them in colorful garments and allowing them to skip school. In a traditional role division, Ruth craves the unconventional, joining her aunt's rebellion, while her sister Lucille conforms. Significantly, Lucille expresses her wish to be "normal" in an obsessive desire to sew clothes exactly like her schoolmates'. She moves in with the Home Economics teacher, selecting a mentor whose occupation contrasts Sylvie's shoddy housekeeping and transience.

Sylvie draws Ruth into her mystical world, inviting her niece to her hideaway, an abandoned house on an island. The dreamlike sequences on and by the water reappropriate the motif of the aunt as an outcast, the recipient of what the heroine is expected to repress or reject. But, whereas in Gaskell's *Mary Barton* the heroine's aunt must die, Aunt Sylvie is not tamed by the men of Fingerbone. She is associated with primal energies and witchcraft (she loves night and the full moon); after initiating the heroine into female mysteries, Sylvie prepares to guide Ruth into the world. When the townspeople threaten to take Ruth away from her aunt, Sylvie sets fire to the house, creating the illusion that the two have died. Transients together, they relinquish their identities and their home as they travel the rails, always on the edge of danger. Sylvie and Ruth have no need to compete with other women, for they want no place in society.

Emma Tennant's *The Bad Sister*, a British novel, is perhaps the most audacious departure from the sister plot of the realistic novel. Tennant relies on Jamesian ambiguities to throw into question the very concept of character as well as notions of "good" and "bad."

Tennant's novel is a collage of various stories, including *The Tempest*, "Cupid and Psyche," and *Jane Eyre*, but most of all it revises Scott's *Heart of Midlothian* and "Cinderella." The body of the text (literally and figuratively, for it will turn up a female corpse) is framed by an "editor's narrative," which ostensibly presents the truth about a popular scandal. The male editor claims to offer a rational and complete version of the story, but, above all, he reveals his total incomprehension of the heroine. Embedded in his initial narrative is another account by a priest who has befriended the heroine. Thus, Tennant creates a situation in which traditional masculine forms of storytelling are in constant dialogue with female narrative strategies; like Elizabeth Jane Howard, she seeks a plot "after" the father's.

The "facts" of the story, as they can be construed, are that a Scotsman named Michael Dalzell fathered a baby in an illicit affair shortly before his wife gave birth to a girl. As a child, the illegitimate Jane Wild shadowed her half sibling. On several occasions, she attempted to hurt her half sister and to embarrass her father. As an adult, Jane Wild has been seen in the company of a woman named Meg, who runs a feminist commune in London. Meg, a friend of and surrogate for Jane's mother ("M for mother, for murder, for Meg. M for her. She made me [Jane] a shadow, discarded," 96), is another of Dalzell's former mistresses. Meg shares the anger of so many of the aunts in traditional sister stories, and she does not limit herself to subtle manipulations in expressing it. Instead, Meg guides Jane in her revenge against the father who deprived her of her inheritance and rightful place in society, the man she perceives as a "symbol of the father of all women" (28). Michael Dalzell and his legitimate daughter (the "good" sister by conventional standards) are assassinated; according to the editor, Jane Wild commits the murders under the "fanatical" (30) influence of Meg.

Seen as a version of Cinderella, Jane is the heroine robbed of her place in the family by her father's marriage, but her behavior more closely resembles that of a cruel stepsister than of the passive Cinderella. Jane feels none of Molly Gibson's guilt and anxiety over her hostility toward her sibling in Gaskell's *Wives and Daughters*. In fact, instead of winning the prince at a ball, Jane kills her sister on the way home from a party. Instead of donning fabulous dancing clothes, she dons male garb. And instead of having a fairy godmother to help her, Jane's mentor is the witchlike Meg, who incorporates aspects of the cruel stepmother. Finally, rather than marrying and living happily ever after, Jane is found dead in the Scottish countryside. Mutilation is not so much the destiny of her rival as the heroine's own fate; she is discovered with a stake through her heart like a vampire, and indeed, throughout, Tennant implies that the half sisters prey on each other.

Seen as a retelling of Scott's historical romance, this work illustrates the effects of an irresponsible nobleman's affair with a woman of lower class. Tennant's heroine, Jane Wild, is divided in her very name; she bears a variant of the appellation of Scott's heroine, Jeanie, and part of the name of his villainess, Madge Wildfire. Tennant's Meg is named after Scott's Madge and her mother, Margaret Murdrockson. In addition, in both books, the illegitimate daughter is possessed by a model of feminine anger; in Scott's novel, the baby is abducted by Madge, and in Tennant's fiction, Jane is controlled by Meg. Tennant further distorts and dislocates the plot of the original by altering the goal of the heroine's quest. Jeanie Deans leaves home to win her half sister's release, whereas Jane Wild travels to assassinate her sibling, thus freeing herself.[8]

The center of the novel consists of Jane's journal, which constantly deviates from the editor's account. Jane drifts in and out of coherence, in and out of time, in and out of her body. She occasionally inhabits an embroidery that depicts a historical romance. In the tapestry, the sisters are pursued by their master, named George after the seducer in *The Heart of Midlothian*. They have been excluded from the "formal" garden (of Eden?) because "we would bring chaos, a bad smell in the place of the polite handkerchief smells" (66). At other times, Jane inserts herself into a version of *The Odyssey*, where she and her sister (rather than the men) are transformed into swine, their sexual urges revealed. Even the "real" world around her appears surrealistic, a city of symbols made concrete. Her apartment adjoins a home for battered women and Paradise Island, a nightclub for lesbians. At Meg's, she waits in a red room that resembles the chamber in the opening of *Jane Eyre*, where another Jane loses control, surrendering to her anger.

Beyond the male "surface" (54), Jane resides in a world of sorcery devoid of distinctions, such as the one between sanity and insanity. She can be suddenly whisked out of her body and into the street, her new form hermaphroditic and swathed in male clothes. With Meg's assistance, she is destroying her old self, abandoning her conventional existence with her boyfriend and his excessively solicitous mother, Mrs. Marten.

Lost in the convolutions of Jane's thought, the reader has no way of knowing what is sheer fantasy. Does the other sister exist? Or is she a figment of Jane's imagination? Certainly, Jane sees herself as double ("Deuter Jane," 95), but she perceives the other as a woman of many guises, as her half sister, as her lover's ex-girlfriend Miranda, as all rivals collectively. Is the editor's narrative Jane's invention, or is she the creation of a mad editor? Does her lover, Tony Marten, exist? Is he different from the devil, Gil-martin, whom Jane joins at the end? The matter is complicated because the entire work is fiction; as when reading *The Turn of the Screw*, one must confront deeply embedded levels of unreality. Discussing characters or parts of characters is virtually impossible.

Jane and her half sister are fused yet distinct. Jane plots revenge on a tormenting sibling, "inside you day and night, enemy or friend, enemy shadow . . . or sister" (83), believing that she can "sample, for a while, the feeling of completeness" (77) without her. The two cannot exist at once; one's life is a threat to the other. But to kill her sister, Jane must extinguish herself. She must "translate" (75) herself into a "sacrifice . . . a living shadow, . . . a drinker of blood, . . . a dark predator or victim . . ." (78). In the end, she has no existence of her own, and she finds only "my terrible absence is there in the glass . . . my non-existence there is almost concrete . . ." (133). Clearly, Tennant offers none of the harmony apparent in the conclusions of novels by Austen, Eliot, Gaskell, Drabble, Pym, or Howard, ambiguous as they might be.

Whereas most of the novels discussed in this study move toward a closed final picture of the heroine, this text starts with the frame (significantly, a male one) and undermines it from within. Tennant ultimately suggests that female character might best be described as a process, not toward a closed or static personality, but constantly in dialectical turmoil. Joining her heroine in asking, "what happened to women, that they were forced into these molds" (130), Tennant proposes an alternative that always "changes and dissolves . . ." (131). Thus, the novel fulfills Jane Gallop's ideal of identity:

> Both psychoanalysis and feminism can be seen as efforts to call into question a rigid identity that cramps and binds. But both also tend to want to produce a "new identity," one that will now be adequate and authentic. I [Gallop] hold the Lacanian view that any identity will necessarily be alien and constraining. . . . Identity must be continually assumed and immediately called into question.[9]

For Tennant's Jane, identity is in fact "alien"; what Meg offers is liberation from her female body and all the "shoulds" imposed by society. She teaches Jane to be a "bad" sister.

By giving up personality as a possession and permitting herself to be possessed, Jane achieves freedom. Abandoning personality as a belonging implicitly involves rejecting role splitting; a quality can no longer belong to one person or another. Moreover, it allows Jane Wild to move freely in and out of sisterhood as she visits her friends Gala and Meg.

It would be contradictory to Tennant's purpose to give this novel a closed reading, to treat it as a solution rather than as a process in itself. In fact, the end is ambiguous. Both sisters are destroyed. Jane is ultimately a corpse, a feminine silence. According to the narrator, in death her face is "completely blank and smooth . . ." (140); by renouncing personality, Jane has erased herself and canceled her text. However, another way of construing her silence is as a feminine cover of coyness, a refusal to participate in a male narrative.

Jane's journal ends with her leaving her body: "I go past so much higher than they . . . I'm pulled by the moon, although it's small and new" (134). She is preparing to meet her demon-lover Gil-martin, a fatherly figure radically different from the patriarchs of the Victorian novel.

Has the bad sister been killed? Or has she merely taken flight?

The unresolved ambiguities at the end of Tennant's novel are full of import for feminists, and especially for literary critics. Tennant's audacious conclusion confronts the difficulty and danger inherent in sisters' development of separate identities. Interpreted in one way, Tennant's novel implies that sisters destroy themselves in their struggle to differentiate and that there is no escaping the damage inflicted by patriarchal authority. Viewed from a different perspective, however, Tennant's story is far more optimistic, suggesting that sisterhood, flight from tradition, and a new kind of heterosexual relationship are possible when women relinquish the entire fiction of character and the illusion that our relations with our sisters (by blood or by choice) are anything but creations of our own minds.

Tennant's novel thus represents the culmination of a long process traced in this book, a process beginning with the pattern derived from the patriarchal tales of Psyche and Cinderella. As we have seen, fictive sisters' relationships have been fraught with anxiety, tension, and even outright hostility, emotions that create discomfort and guilt in the heroines and ultimately affect other aspects of their lives, including courtship and marriage.

The nineteenth-century novels I have discussed illustrate the increasing isolation of the heroine as a result of role splitting. In Austen's books, role splitting is seen as a necessary part of a conclusion that divides the sisters along class or geographical boundaries, thus eliminating competition. Gaskell, on the other hand, reveals how sisters' insistence on differences can keep them interdependent and bound to the paternal home, and she offers the alternative of a sisterhood based on similarities among unrelated women. Gaskell's alternative coexists with the patriarchal sister story and remains threatened by it. Eliot, too, shows the pain and danger resulting from role splitting, and her vision is even more negative than Gaskell's. Instead of offering the possibility of sisterhood, tenuous as it might be, she suggests that divisions between sisters must be accompanied by their isolation from peers. The solution Eliot offers, which involves one sister relinquishing personality and the other accepting her similarities to her sister, is mixed at best.

Confronted with such pessimism, more recent writers have felt compelled to revise their sister authors' plots as well as the sister story inherited from patriarchal tradition. Their struggle to come to terms with male and female traditions is apparent in strained coincidences and a stretching of the conventions of the realistic novel. Moreover, the growing significance of issues involving sisters and sisterhood is signaled by an emphasis on relationships involving women, which compete with heterosexual romances for readers' attention. Barbara Pym depicts a world in which harmony among biological siblings is purchased at the expense of sisterhood. She presents a marked contrast to Elizabeth Gaskell, whose works she most consciously revises, and who perceives sisters and sisterhood as coexisting. Elizabeth Jane Howard, too, indicates that sisterly solidarity excludes sisterhood. Furthermore, she suggests that one remedy for the divisions created by role splitting is for sisters to reverse roles and to accept one another's qualities. At the same time, Howard shows the difficulties in finding a plot "after" the father's, a concern that preoccupies Drabble as well, as her heroine strives to resolve contradictory impulses toward closeness and distance. Overshadowing Drabble's heroine are outworn notions of "good" or appropriate behavior inherited from earlier fictions; before her characters can come to terms with themselves and each other, they must accept the uselessness of these perconceptions. Drabble emphasizes what is implicit in earlier works: that sisters by blood or by choice are our creations, and that the rejection of role splitting is essential to achieving an integrated personality. Finally, Emma Tennant goes beyond Drabble, questioning personality itself and ultimately rejecting it. Like the conventions of realistic fiction, she considers personality a patriarchal constraint preventing women from perceiving possibilities for recreating their stories.

As I have shown, the range and development in these sister stories is at odds with much contemporary criticism. Many articles and books by women idealize sisterhoods and gloss over tense bonds between biological sisters. Others avoid dealing with biological sisters in a systematic fashion, obscuring the persistent friction and problems with individuation in such relationships. Feminist criticism has opened up novels by women in innovative and exciting ways, and without it, this book could never have been conceived or completed. Yet critical discomfort with biological sisters is an expression of a dilemma experienced by women today, one that pits a political desire for harmony against the realities of conflicting viewpoints and preferences. As Elizabeth Jane Howard has shown, we cannot rewrite the father's story, and although we may send the mother upstairs with Jane Austen, she remains in the house. Similarly, we cannot divorce ourselves from our sisters.

But we can write, and, as Emma Tennant illustrates in Jane Wild's journal, we can write ourselves out of constructs of personality, which are, after all, nothing but fictions. Jane Wild (together with her creator) rejects the safe frame of a conventional closure; she refuses to leave us with a concluding marriage or an idealized picture of women sitting together around a hearth. By revising her story in a way that welcomes danger, ambiguity, and intrigue, Jane Wild offers the possibility of evading conventional constraints. Despite the male editor's doubts, she believes that women can take flight—and so we might.

Notes

Chapter 1. Introduction: Blossoms on One Stem

1. See Louisa May Alcott, *Little Women* (New York: Grosset and Dunlap, 1947).

2. Louise Bernikow, *Among Women* (New York: Harper, 1980), 74.

3. Wilkie Collins, *No Name* (New York: Dover, 1978) and *The Woman in White* (New York: Dutton, 1969); Jane Austen, *Pride and Prejudice*, vol. 2 of *The Novels of Jane Austen*, ed. R. W. Chapman (London: Oxford University Press, 1965); Margaret Mitchell, *Gone with the Wind* (New York: Macmillan, 1936). All subsequent quotations from *Pride and Prejudice* will be cited parenthetically in the text.

4. Antonia Byatt, *Still Life* (New York: Scribner, 1985); Rebecca West, *The Fountain Overflows* (New York: Viking, 1956); Elizabeth Gaskell, *Wives and Daughters* (New York: Penguin, 1976); Gail Godwin, *A Mother and Two Daughters* (New York: Avon, 1982) and *The Odd Woman* (New York: Warner, 1974); Marilynne Robinson, *Housekeeping* (New York: Farrar, Straus, and Giroux, 1980); and Alice Walker, *The Color Purple* (New York: Washington Square Press, 1982).

5. Toni McNaron, ed., *The Sister Bond: A Feminist View of a Timeless Connection* (New York: Pergamon, 1985); Susan Lanser, "No Connections Subsequent: Jane Austen's World of Sisterhood," in McNaron, *The Sister Bond*, 51–67; Bernikow, *Among Women*, 74–109; Christine Downing, *Psyche's Sisters: Reimagining the Meaning of Sisterhood* (New York: Harper, 1988); Elizabeth Fishel, *Sisters* (New York: William Morrow, 1979); Dale Atkins, *Sisters* (New York: Arbor, 1984); Carol Lasser, " 'Let Us Be Sisters Forever': The Sororal Model of Nineteenth-Century Female Friendship," *Signs* 14 (1988): 158–81.

6. Patricia Meyer Spacks, "Sisters," in *Fetter'd or Free? British Women Novelists, 1670–1815*, ed. Mary Anne Schofield and Cecelia Macheski (Athens: Ohio University Press, 1986), 136–51.

7. Glenda Ann Hudson, "Sibling Relationships in Jane Austen's Fiction" (Ph.D. diss., Vanderbilt University, 1987).

8. Joanne Creighton, "Sisterly Symbiosis: Margaret Drabble's *The Waterfall* and A. S. Byatt's *The Game*," *Mosaic* 20 (1987): 15–20.

9. Rhoda Irene Sherwood, " 'A Special Kind of Double': Sisters in British and American Fiction" (Ph.D. diss., University of Wisconsin—Milwaukee, 1987).

10. Nina Auerbach, *Communities of Women: An Idea in Fiction* (Cambridge: Harvard University Press, 1978), 3–4.

11. Paul Ricoeur, "The Metaphorical Process as Cognition, Imagination, and Feeling," in *On Metaphor*, ed. Sheldon Sacks (Chicago: University of Chicago Press, 1979), 151.

12. Jacques Derrida, "White Mythology: Metaphor in the Text of Philosophy," in *Margins of Philosophy*, trans. Alan Bass (Chicago: University of Chicago Press, 1982), 211.

13. Ibid., 241–43.

14. Tillie Olsen, *Silences* (New York: Delacorte, 1978).

15. George W. F. Hegel, *The Phenomenology of the Mind*, trans. and intro. J. B. Baillie (New York: Harper, 1967), 475–99.

16. Christina Rossetti, "Goblin Market," in *Poems* (London: Macmillan, 1891), 11.

17. Ibid., 7.

18. Bernikow, *Among Women*, 99.

19. Jane Gallop, *The Daughter's Seduction: Feminism and Psychoanalysis* (Ithaca: Cornell University Press, 1982); Juliet Mitchell, *Psychoanalysis and Feminism* (New York: Random House, 1974).

20. Downing, *Psyche's Sisters*, 12.

21. Bernikow, *Among Women*, 19.

22. Toni McNaron, "How Little We Know and How Much We Feel," in *The Sister Bond*, ed. McNaron, 8.

23. *The Female Aegis, or, The Duties of Women*, ed. Gina Luria (New York: Garland, 1974), 148.

24. Downing, *Psyche's Sisters*, 168.

25. Bernikow, *Among Women*, 144.

26. Carroll Smith-Rosenberg, "The Female World of Love and Ritual," in *A Heritage of Her Own*, ed. Nancy F. Cott and Elizabeth H. Peck (New York: Simon and Schuster, 1979), 325.

27. Lasser, " 'Let Us Be Sisters Forever,' " 163–79.

28. Luise Eichenbaum and Susie Orbach, *Between Women: Love, Envy, and Competition in Women's Friendships* (New York: Viking, 1988), 21.

29. Atkins, *Sisters*, 14.

30. Tony Tanner, *Adultery in the Novel: Contract and Transgression* (Baltimore: Johns Hopkins University Press, 1979), 12.

31. McNaron, "How Little We Know," 7.

32. Hélène Cixous, "The Character of 'Character,' " trans. Keith Cohen, *New Literary History* 5 (1974): 309.

33. Robert Highbie, *Character and Structure in the English Novel* (Gainesville: University of Florida Press, 1984), 17.

34. Adrienne Rich, *On Lies, Secrets, and Silence: Selected Prose 1966–1979* (New York: Norton, 1979), 39.

35. West, *The Fountain Overflows*, 132.

36. Bruno Bettleheim, *The Uses of Enchantment* (New York: Vintage, 1977), 9.

37. Fishel, *Sisters*, 181.

38. In her discussion of fairy-tale sisters, Christine Downing distinguishes between the "polarity plot" and the "complementarity plot" (*Psyche's Sisters*, 30), but, in fact, they are one. Sisters who are opposites are complementary.

39. Patsy Stoneman, *Elizabeth Gaskell* (Bloomington: Indiana University Press, 1987), 187.

40. Auerbach, *Communities of Women*, 8.

41. Erich Neumann, *Amor and Psyche: The Psychic Development of the Feminine. A Commentary on the Tale by Apuleius*, trans. Ralph Manheim, Bollingen Series, vol. 54 (Princeton: Princeton University Press, 1971), 73.

42. Ibid., 12.

43. C. S. Lewis retells the story from the perspective of Psyche's eldest sister in *Till We Have Faces, A Myth Retold* (New York: Harcourt, 1956). He, too, shows the sister's hostility as rooted in love and loss; he mitigates the homosexual and incestuous nature of the relationship by turning the sister into a warrior and ruler, thus denying her femininity.

44. Neumann, *Amor and Psyche*, 74.

45. Carolyn Heilbrun, *Reinventing Womanhood* (New York: Norton, 1979), 143.

46. Fishel, *Sisters*, 159.

47. Bettleheim, *The Uses of Enchantment*, 26.

48. Jack Zipes, *The Brothers Grimm: From Enchanted Forest to the Modern World* (New York: Routledge, 1988), 141.

49. Ibid., 24.

50. Marianne Hirsch, "Spiritual *Bildung:* The Beautiful Soul as Paradigm," in *The Voyage In: Fictions of Female Development*, ed. Elizabeth Abel et al. (Hanover, N.H.: University Press of New England, 1983), 24.

51. Downing, *Psyche's Sisters*, 83.

52. George Eliot, *Middlemarch*, ed. Bert G. Hornback (New York: Norton, 1977), 577. All subsequent quotations from this work will be cited parenthetically in the text.

53. In *Women's Fiction, A Guide to Novels by and about Women in America, 1820–1870* (Ithaca: Cornell University Press, 1978), Nina Baym comments on similar plots in American novels, noting that "most guilty [of tormenting the heroine] are aunts, usually the mother's sisters" (37).

54. Sandra M. Gilbert and Susan Gubar, *The Madwoman in the Attic: The Woman Writer and the Nineteenth-Century Literary Imagination* (New Haven: Yale University Press, 1979), 173.

55. Harriet Martineau, *Deerbrook* (Garden City: Dial-Virago, 1984); Christina Rossetti, "Goblin Market"; Charlotte Brontë, *Jane Eyre* (Harmondsworth, England: Penguin, 1971).

56. Charlotte Brontë, *Villette* (New York: Dutton, 1957), and *Shirley* (London: J. M. Dent, 1969).

57. George Gissing, *The Odd Women* (New York: Norton, 1971).

58. Bernikow, *Among Women*, 77.

59. Nancy Miller, *Subject to Change: Reading Feminist Writing* (New York: Columbia University Press, 1986), 356.

60. Downing, *Psyche's Sisters*, 4.

Chapter 2. Jane Austen: The Sister Plots

1. Jane Austen, *Selected Letters*, ed. R. W. Chapman (London: Oxford University Press, 1985), 208.

2. Lanser, "No Connections Subsequent," 54.

3. Geoffrey Gorer, "Poor Honey: Some Notes on Jane Austen and Her Mother," *London Magazine* 4 (1957): 35–48.

4. Hudson, "Sibling Relationships in Jane Austen's Fiction."

5. Jane Austen, *The Watsons*, in *Minor Works*, vol. 6 of *The Novels of Jane Austen*, ed. R. W. Chapman (London: Oxford University Press, 1965), 118.

6. Jane Austen, *Lesley Castle*, in *Minor Works*, 113.

7. Auerbach, *Communities of Women*, 46; Patricia Beer, *Reader I Married Him: A Study of the Women Characters of Jane Austen, Charlotte Brontë, Elizabeth Gaskell, and George Eliot* (New York: Barnes and Noble, 1974), 76.

8. Jane Austen, *The Three Sisters*, in *Minor Works*, 64.

9. Samuel Butler, *The Way of All Flesh* (New York: Dutton, 1916), 43.

10. See, for instance, Kenneth Moler, *Jane Austen's Art of Allusion* (Lincoln: University of Nebraska Press, 1969), 43–73.

11. Tony Tanner, *Jane Austen* (Cambridge: Harvard University Press, 1986), 99.

12. Jane Austen, *Sense and Sensibility*, vol. 1 of *The Novels of Jane Austen*, ed. R. W. Chapman (London: Oxford University Press, 1960), 6. All subsequent quotations from this work will be cited parenthetically in the text.

13. Stephen Bank and Michael D. Kahn, *The Sibling Bond* (New York: Basic Books, 1982), 110–11.

14. Jane Nardin, *Those Elegant Decorums: The Concept of Propriety in Jane Austen's Novels* (Albany: State University of New York Press, 1973), 36.

15. Suzanne Juhasz, "Facilitating Environments," unpublished manuscript, 32.

16. Susan Morgan, "Polite Lies: The Veiled Heroine of *Sense and Sensibility*," *Nineteenth-Century Fiction* 31 (1976): 204–5.

17. Dennis Allen, "No Love for Lydia: The Fate of Desire in *Pride and Prejudice*," *Texas Studies in Language and Literature* 24 (1985): 430.

18. Spacks, "Sisters," 137.

19. Bank and Kahn, *The Sibling Bond*, 50.

20. Ibid., 51.

21. Rachel Brownstein, *Becoming a Heroine* (New York: Penguin, 1984), 108.

22. Fishel, *Sisters*, 153.

23. Françoise Basch, *Relative Creatures: Victorian Women in Society and the Novel* (New York: Schocken, 1974), 271.

24. James Twitchell, *Forbidden Partners: The Incest Taboo in Modern Culture* (New York: Columbia University Press, 1982), 9.

25. Hudson, "Sibling Relationships in Jane Austen's Fiction," 27.

26. Brownstein, *Becoming a Heroine*, 102.

27. Jane Austen, *Persuasion*, vol. 5 of *The Novels of Jane Austen*, ed. R. W. Chapman (London: Oxford University Press, 1965), 5. All subsequent quotations from this work will be cited parenthetically in the text.

28. Lanser, "No Connections Subsequent," 54.

29. Tanner, *Jane Austen*, 209.

30. Nardin, *Those Elegant Decorums*, 142.

31. Leo Bersani, *A Future for Astyanax: Character and Desire in Literature* (New York: Columbia University Press, 1984), 76.

32. Jane Austen, *Mansfield Park*, vol. 3 of *The Novels of Jane Austen*, ed. R. W. Chapman (London: Oxford University Press, 1960), 10.

33. R. F. Brissenden, "*Mansfield Park:* Freedom and the Family," in *Jane Austen: Bicentenary Essays*, ed. John Halperin (New York: Cambridge University Press, 1975), 165.

34. Gilbert and Gubar, *The Madwoman in the Attic*, 158.

35. Susan Siefert, *The Dilemma of the Talented Heroine: A Study in Nineteenth-Century Fiction* (Montreal: Eden, 1977), 80.

36. Jane Austen, *Emma*, vol. 4 of *The Novels of Jane Austen*, ed. R. W. Chapman (London: Oxford University Press, 1960), 166.

Chapter 3. Elizabeth Gaskell: Embroidering the Pattern

1. Bank and Kahn, *The Sibling Bond*, 50.

2. Arnold Rotner, "Mrs. Gaskell's Art" (Ph.D. diss., University of Colorado, 1967), 192.

3. *The Letters of Mrs. Gaskell*, ed. J. A. V. Chapple and Arthur Pollard (Cambridge: Harvard University Press, 1967), 435.

4. Edgar Wright, *Mrs. Gaskell: The Basis for Reassessment* (New York: Oxford University Press, 1965), 53.

5. David Cecil, *Victorian Novelists* (Chicago: University of Chicago Press, 1958), 186.

6. Coral Lansbury, *Elizabeth Gaskell: The Novel of Social Crisis* (London: Paul Elek, 1975), 8.

7. Elizabeth Gaskell, *Mary Barton* (New York: Penguin, 1984), 43. All subsequent quotations from this work will be cited parenthetically in the text.

8. Elizabeth Gaskell, "Mr. Harrison's Confessions," in vol. 5 of *The Works of Mrs. Gaskell* (New York: Putnam 1906), 450. All subsequent quotations from this work will be cited parenthetically in the text.

9. Auerbach, *Communities of Women*, 80.

10. Elizabeth Gaskell, *Cranford*, in *Cranford/Cousin Phillis* (New York: Penguin, 1982), 88. All subsequent quotations from this work will be cited parenthetically in the text.

11. Stoneman, *Elizabeth Gaskell*, 89.

12. Martin Dodsworth, "Women Without Men at Cranford," *Essays in Criticism* 13 (1963): 138.

13. Ibid., 133.

14. Auerbach, *Communities of Women*, 87.

15. Coral Lansbury, *Elizabeth Gaskell* (Boston: Twayne, 1984), 74.

16. Thomas P. Fair, "The Paternal Model in the Novels of Elizabeth Gaskell" (Ph.D. diss., University of Colorado, 1986), 104.

17. Auerbach, *Communities of Women*, 82.

18. Ibid., 80–87.

19. Elizabeth Gaskell, *Wives and Daughters* (New York: Penguin, 1976), 58. All subsequent quotations from this work will be cited parenthetically in the text.

20. Angus Easson, *Elizabeth Gaskell* (London: Routledge and Kegan Paul, 1979), 194.

21. Ibid.

22. Lansbury, *Elizabeth Gaskell: The Novel of Social Crisis*, 199.

23. Stoneman, *Elizabeth Gaskell*, 180.

24. See, for instance, Arthur Pollard, *Mrs. Gaskell: Novelist and Biographer* (Cambridge: Harvard University Press, 1966), 232.

25. *The Letters of Mrs. Gaskell*, 731.

26. Patricia Meyer Spacks, *The Female Imagination* (New York: Knopf, 1975), 93.

27. Jacqueline Berke and Laura Berke, "Mothers and Daughters in *Wives and Daughters:* A Study of Gaskell's Last Novel," in *The Lost Tradition: Mothers and Daughters in Literature*, ed. Cathy N. Davidson and E. M. Broner (New York: Frederick Ungar, 1980), 100.

28. Lansbury, *Elizabeth Gaskell*, 113.

29. Stoneman, *Elizabeth Gaskell*, 187.

30. Gallop, *The Daughter's Seduction*, 76.

31. Patricia Meyer Spacks, *The Adolescent Idea: Myths of Youth and the Adult Imagination* (New York: Harper, 1986), 36.

32. Arthur Pollard, *Mrs. Gaskell: Novelist and Biographer*, 159.

33. Winifred Gérin, *Elizabeth Gaskell: A Biography* (Oxford: Oxford University Press, 1976), 167.

34. Elizabeth Gaskell, *The Life of Charlotte Brontë* (New York: Penguin, 1975), 55. All subsequent quotations from this work will be cited parenthetically in the text.

35. Alan Shelston, introduction to *The Life of Charlotte Brontë*, by Elizabeth Gaskell, 28–29.

36. Ibid., 26.

37. Lansbury, *Elizabeth Gaskell: The Novel of Social Crisis*, 147.

38. Auerbach, *Communities of Women*, 93.

39. Although this closeness between Anne and Emily may have existed more in Gaskell's imagination than in actuality, it might also exemplify a particular type of psychological bonding among siblings. Whereas such authors as Austen and Gaskell have emphasized differences between sisters in their fictional characters, certain psychologists, such as Heinz Kohut, Marjorie Taggart White, and Marcella Baker Weiner, have theorized about a "twinship transference." Kohut's philosophy is explained in his book, *How Does Analysis Cure?*, ed. Arnold Goldberg (Chicago: University of Chicago Press, 1984), while White and Weiner's ideas are developed in *The Theory and Practice of Self Psychology* (New York: Brunner-Mazel, 1986). Based on "shared skills, talents and experiences" (White and Weiner, 105), "twinship" arises when other forms of transference fail for an individual, and it is a "compensatory structure" (White and Weiner, 114). For Anne and Emily Brontë, for instance, the lack of opportunities to develop transference through their parents may have led to just such a "twinship" of near total empathy and undifferentiated emotions.

40. Nina Auerbach, *Woman and the Demon: The Life of a Victorian Myth* (Cambridge: Harvard University Press, 1982), 127.

41. Suzann Bick, "Clouding the 'Severe Truth': Elizabeth Gaskell's Strategy in *The Life of Charlotte Brontë*," *Essays in Arts and Sciences* 1 (1982): 38.

42. Lansbury, *Elizabeth Gaskell*, 87.

43. Gérin, *Elizabeth Gaskell: A Biography*, 171.

44. Bick, "Clouding the 'Severe Truth,'" 35.

45. Yvonne Ffrench, *Mrs. Gaskell* (Denver: Alan Swallow, 1949), 36.

46. Auerbach, *Communities of Women*, 91.

47. Ibid., 93.

48. Ibid., 96.

Chapter 4. George Eliot: Superfluous Sisters

1. Ruby Redinger, *George Eliot: The Emergent Self* (New York: Knopf, 1975), 166, 175.

2. Jenni Calder, *Women and Marriage in Victorian Fiction* (New York: Oxford University Press, 1976), 125.

3. George Eliot, *The Mill on the Floss*, ed. A. S. Byatt (Harmondsworth, England: Penguin, 1979), 109. All subsequent quotations from this work will be cited parenthetically in the text.

4. Nina Auerbach, *Romantic Imprisonment: Women and Other Glorified Outcasts* (New York: Columbia University Press, 1985), 237.

5. Ellen Moers, *Literary Women* (Garden City, New York: Doubleday, 1976), 194–95; Lee Edwards, "Women, Energy, and *Middlemarch*," in *Middlemarch*, by George Eliot, 685; Beer, *Reader, I Married Him*, 196.

6. See, for instance, Redinger, *George Eliot: The Emergent Self*, 469; Siefert, *The Dilemma of the Talented Heroine*, 16; and "*Middlemarch*," in *Middlemarch*, by George Eliot, 646.

7. Moers, *Literary Women*, 194.

8. Robert Coles, *Irony in the Mind's Eye: Essays on Novels by James Agee, Elizabeth Bowen, and George Eliot* (New York: New Directions, 1974), 175.

9. George Eliot, *Daniel Deronda*, ed. Barbara Hardy (Harmondsworth, England: Penguin, 1967), 53. All subsequent quotations from this work will be cited parenthetically in the text.

10. Brownstein, *Becoming a Heroine*, 101.

11. Redinger, *George Eliot: The Emergent Self,* 475.

12. Brownstein, *Becoming a Heroine*, 211n.

13. Bonnie Zimmerman, "Gwendolen Harleth and 'The Girl of the Period,'" in *George Eliot: Centenary Essays and an Unpublished Fragment,* ed. Anne Smith (London: Vision, 1980), 214.

Chapter 5. Pym, Howard, and Drabble: Revising the Sister

1. Robert Long, *Barbara Pym* (New York: Ungar, 1986), 210; Margaret Ezell, "'What Shall We Do With Our Old Maids': Barbara Pym and the 'Woman Question,'" *International Journal of Women's Studies* 7 (1984): 456; Gail Cunningham, "Women and Children First: The Novels of Margaret Drabble," in *Twentieth-Century Women Novelists,* ed. Thomas Staley (Totowa, N.J.: Barnes and Noble, 1982), 131.

2. Margaret Drabble, *A Summer Bird-Cage* (Harmondsworth, England: Penguin, 1971), 68. All subsequent quotations from this work will be cited parenthetically in the text.

3. Elizabeth Jane Howard, *After Julius* (New York: Harper, 1982), 140. All subsequent quotations from this work will be cited parenthetically in the text.

4. For Pym's comments, see Robert Long, *Barbara Pym*, 201. Margaret Drabble's remarks on Eliot appear in Nancy Poland, "Margaret Drabble: 'There Must Be a Lot of People Like Me,'" *Midwest Quarterly* 16 (1975): 256, and Barbara Milton, "The Art of Fiction LXX," *Paris Review,* 20, no. 74 (1978): 52. Drabble's remarks on Elizabeth Gaskell appear in Milton, "The Art of Fiction," 52, and Diana Cooper-Clark, "Margaret Drabble: Cautious Feminist," *Atlantic Monthly* 246 (November 1980): 72.

5. Sandra M. Gilbert and Susan Gubar, *The War of the Words,* vol. 1 of *No Man's Land: The Place of the Woman Writer in the Twentieth Century* (New Haven: Yale University Press, 1988), 208.

6. Janice Rossen, *The World of Barbara Pym* (New York: St. Martin's Press, 1987), 9.

7. Peter Firchow, "Margaret Drabble," in *The Writer's Place: Interviews on the Literary Situation in Contemporary Britain,* ed. Peter Firchow (Minneapolis: University of Minnesota Press, 1975), 106.

8. Margaret Drabble, personal interview with the author, 29 December 1988.

9. Firchow, "Margaret Drabble," 121.

10. Arnold Davidson, "Pride and Prejudice in Margaret Drabble's *A Summer Bird-Cage,*" *Arizona Quarterly* 38 (1982): 306–7.

11. Joanne Creighton, *Margaret Drabble* (London: Methuen, 1985), 8.

12. Long, *Barbara Pym*, 25; Frederick Keener, "Barbara Pym Herself and Jane Austen," *Twentieth-Century Literature* 31 (1985): 93.

13. Long, *Barbara Pym*, 26.

14. Barbara Pym, *Some Tame Gazelle* (New York: Harper, 1984), 16. All subsequent quotations from this work will be cited parenthetically in the text.

15. Jane Nardin, *Barbara Pym* (Boston: Twayne, 1985), 66.

16. Diana Benet, *Something to Love: Barbara Pym's Novels* (Columbia: University of Missouri Press, 1986), 27.

17. Ibid., 22.

18. Ibid., 27.

19. Ibid.

20. John Bayley, "Where, Exactly, is the Pym World?" in *The Life and Work of Barbara Pym*, ed. Dale Salwak (London: Macmillan, 1987), 53.

21. Long, *Barbara Pym*, 39.

22. Ibid., 38.

23. Benet, *Something to Love*, 16.

24. Nardin, *Barbara Pym*, 71.

25. Rossen, *The World of Barbara Pym*, 59.

26. Sherwood, "'A Special Kind of Double,'" 134.

27. Barbara Pym, *An Unsuitable Attachment* (New York: Harper, 1983), 25. All subsequent quotations from this work will be cited parenthetically in the text.

28. Ezell, "'What Shall We Do With Our Old Maids,'" 462.

29. Benet, *Something to Love*, 107.

30. Milton, "The Art of Fiction," 54.

31. Margaret Drabble, personal interview with the author, 29 December 1988.

32. See Antonia S. Byatt, *The Game* (New York: Scribner, 1967), and *Still Life* (New York: Scribner, 1985).

33. Creighton, "Sisterly Symbiosis," 23.

34. Arnold Davidson, "Pride and Prejudice," 303–4.

35. Bernard Bergonzi, *The Situation of the Novel* (London: Macmillan, 1970), 22.

36. Susanna Roxman, *Guilt and Glory: Studies in Margaret Drabble's Novels, 1963–1980* (Stockholm: Almquist and Wiksell, 1984), 16.

37. Joan Manheimer, "Margaret Drabble and the Journey to the Self," *Studies in the Literary Imagination* 11 (1978): 130.

38. Virginia Beards, "Margaret Drabble: Novels of a Cautionary Feminist," *Critique* 15 (1973): 42.

39. Ellen C. Rose, "Margaret Drabble: Surviving the Future," *Critique* 15 (1973): 5.

40. Creighton, *Margaret Drabble*, 40. Emphasis added.

41. Elizabeth Fox-Genovese, "The Ambiguities of Female Identity: A Reading of the Novels of Margaret Drabble," *Partisan Review* 46 (1979): 247.

42. Manheimer, "Margaret Drabble and the Journey to the Self," 128.

43. Ibid.

44. Arnold Davidson, "Pride and Prejudice," 310.

45. Sherwood, "'A Special Kind of Double,'" 81.

46. Fox-Genovese, "The Ambiguities of Female Identity," 246.

47. Helena Michie, "Mother, Sister, Other: The 'Other' Woman in Feminist Theory," *Literature and Psychology* 32, no. 4 (1986): 2.

Chapter 6. Conclusion: Killing the Good Sister; or, The Return of the Witch

1. Eichenbaum and Orbach, *Between Women*, 32.

2. For information on the following works, see chapter 1, note 4: Robinson, *Housekeeping;* Godwin, *A Mother and Two Daughters* and *The Odd Woman;* Walker, *The Color Purple*. See also Judith Rossner, *His Little Women* (New York: Simon and Schuster, 1990); Nancy Thayer, *Three Women at the Water's Edge* (New York: Bantam, 1983); Emma Tennant, *The Bad Sister* (London: Pan, 1983). All subsequent quotations from Tennant's *The Bad Sister* will be cited parenthetically in the text.

3. Toni Morrison, *Sula* (New York: Knopf, 1974).

4. Walker, *The Color Purple*, 146.

5. Ibid., 198.

6. Robinson, *Housekeeping*, 53.

7. Ibid., 3.

8. For additional details, see Sir Walter Scott, *The Heart of Midlothian* (New York: Penguin, 1984).

9. Gallop, *The Daughter's Seduction*, xii.

Bibliography

Novels and Short Stories

Alcott, Louisa May. *Little Women*. New York: Grosset and Dunlap, 1947.

Austen, Jane. *Emma*. Edited by R. W. Chapman. Vol. 4 of *The Novels of Jane Austen*. London: Oxford University Press, 1960.

———. *Mansfield Park*. Edited by R. W. Chapman. Vol. 3 of *The Novels of Jane Austen*. London: Oxford University Press, 1960.

———. *Minor Works*. Edited by R. W. Chapman. Vol. 6 of *The Novels of Jane Austen*. London: Oxford University Press, 1965.

———. *Persuasion*. Edited by R. W. Chapman. Vol. 5 of *The Novels of Jane Austen*. London: Oxford University Press, 1965.

———. *Pride and Prejudice*. Edited by R. W. Chapman. Vol. 2 of *The Novels of Jane Austen*. London: Oxford University Press, 1965.

———. *Sense and Sensibility*. Edited by R. W. Chapman. Vol. 1 of *The Novels of Jane Austen*. London: Oxford University Press, 1960.

Austen, Jane, and Another Lady. *Sanditon*. Boston: Houghton Mifflin, 1975.

Booth, Pat. *The Sisters*. New York: Crown, 1987.

Bowles, Jane. "Camp Cataract." In *My Sister's Hand in Mine: The Collected Works of Jane Bowles*, 359–401. New York: Ecco, 1977.

Brontë, Charlotte. *Jane Eyre*. Harmondsworth, England: Penguin, 1971.

———. *Villette*. New York: Dutton, 1957.

Butler, Samuel. *The Way of All Flesh*. New York: Dutton, 1916.

Byatt, Antonia S. *The Game*. New York: Scribner, 1967.

———. *Still Life*. New York: Scribner, 1985.

Cahill, Susan, ed. *Among Sisters: Short Stories by Women Writers*. New York: New American Library, 1989.

Chase, Joan. *During the Reign of the Queen of Persia*. New York: Harper and Row, 1983.

Collins, Wilkie. *No Name*. Dover, 1978.

———. *The Woman in White*. New York: Dutton, 1969.

Dickens, Charles. *Little Dorrit*. Harmondsworth, England: Penguin, 1975.

Drabble, Margaret. *A Summer Bird-Cage*. Harmondsworth, England: Penguin, 1971.

———. *The Waterfall*. Harmondsworth, England: Penguin, 1971.

Eliot, George. *Daniel Deronda*. Edited by Barbara Hardy. Harmondsworth, England: Penguin, 1967.

———. *Middlemarch*. Edited by Bert G. Hornback. New York: Norton, 1977.

——. *The Mill on the Floss*. Edited by A. S. Byatt. Harmondsworth, England: Penguin, 1979.

Forster, E. M. *Howard's End*. New York: Vintage, 1955.

Gaskell, Elizabeth. *Cranford/Cousin Phillis*. New York: Penguin, 1982.

——. "The Half-Brothers." In vol. 5 of *The Works of Mrs. Gaskell*, 391–404. New York: Putnam, 1906.

——. *Mary Barton*. New York: Penguin, 1984.

——. "Mr. Harrison's Confessions." In vol. 5 of *The Works of Mrs. Gaskell*, 405–91. New York: Putnam, 1906.

——. *Wives and Daughters*. New York: Penguin, 1976.

Gissing, George. *The Odd Women*. New York: Norton, 1971.

Godwin, Gail. *A Mother and Two Daughters*. New York: Avon, 1982.

——. *The Odd Woman*. New York: Warner, 1974.

Hardy, Thomas. *Tess of the D'Urbervilles*. New York: Norton, 1978.

Hazzard, Shirley. *The Transit of Venus*. New York: Viking, 1980.

Holden, Ursula. *Wider Pools*. London: Methuen, 1983.

Howard, Elizabeth Jane. *After Julius*. New York: Harper, 1982.

Lawrence, D. H. *Women in Love*. New York: Modern Library, 1977.

Lessing, Doris. *The Fifth Child*. New York: Knopf, 1988.

Lewis, C. S. *Till We Have Faces, A Myth Retold*. New York: Harcourt, 1956.

Mansfield, Katherine. "The Daughters of the Late Colonel." In *The Garden Party*, 88–119. Harmondsworth, England: Penguin, 1962.

Martineau, Harriet. *Deerbrook*. Garden City: Dial-Virago, 1984.

Mitchell, Margaret. *Gone with the Wind*. New York: Macmillan, 1936.

Morrison, Toni. *Sula*. New York: Knopf, 1974.

Oates, Joyce Carol. *The Bloodsmoor Romance*. New York: Warner, 1982.

Pym, Barbara. *Some Tame Gazelle*. New York: Harper, 1984.

——. *An Unsuitable Attachment*. New York: Harper, 1983.

Robertson, E. Arnot. *Ordinary Families*. New York: Dial-Virago, 1982.

Robinson, Marilynne. *Housekeeping*. New York: Farrar, Straus, Giroux, 1980.

Rossner, Judith. *His Little Women*. New York: Simon and Schuster, 1990.

Scott, Sir Walter. *The Heart of Midlothian*. New York: Penguin, 1984.

Sinclair, May. *The Three Sisters*. London: Virago, 1982.

Taylor, Elizabeth. *The Sleeping Beauty*. New York: Dial-Virago, 1975.

Tennant, Emma. *The Bad Sister*. London: Pan, 1983.

Thayer, Nancy. *Three Women at the Water's Edge*. New York: Bantam, 1983.

Trollope, Anthony. *The Claverings*. New York: Dover, 1977.

Walker, Alice. *The Color Purple*. New York: Washington Square Press, 1982.

West, Rebecca. *The Fountain Overflows*. New York: Viking, 1956.

Wittig, Monique. *Les Guerillères*. Translated by David Le Vay. London: Owen, 1971.

Other Works

Abel, Elizabeth, Marianne Hirsch, and Elizabeth Langland, eds. *The Voyage In: Fictions of Female Development*. Hanover, N.H.: University Press of New England, 1983.

Abbott, H. Porter. "Saul Bellow and the Lost Cause of Character." *Novel* 13 (1980): 264–83.

Alaya, Flavia. "Feminists on Victorians: The Pardoning Frame of Mind." *Dickens Studies Annual: Essays on Victorian Fiction* 15 (1986): 337–80.

Allen, Dennis W. "No Love for Lydia: The Fate of Desire in *Pride and Prejudice*." *Texas Studies in Language and Literature* 24 (1985): 425–43.

Armens, Sven. *Archetypes of the Family in Literature*. Seattle: University of Washington Press, 1966.

Armstrong, Nancy. *Desire and Domestic Fiction: A Political History of the Novel*. New York: Oxford University Press, 1987.

Atkins, Dale V. *Sisters*. New York: Arbor, 1984.

Auerbach, Nina. *Communities of Women: An Idea in Fiction*. Cambridge: Harvard University Press, 1978.

———. *Romantic Imprisonment: Women and Other Glorified Outcasts*. New York: Columbia University Press, 1985.

———. *Woman and the Demon: The Life of a Victorian Myth*. Cambridge: Harvard University Press, 1982.

Austen, Jane. *Selected Letters*. Edited by R. W. Chapman. London: Oxford University Press, 1985.

Auster, Henry. "George Eliot and the Modern Temper." In *The Worlds of Victorian Fiction*, edited by Jerome Buckley, 75–102.

Bank, Stephen P., and Michael D. Kahn. *The Sibling Bond*. New York: Basic Books, 1982.

Basch, Françoise. *Relative Creatures: Victorian Women in Society and the Novel*. New York: Schocken, 1974.

Bayley, John. "Where, Exactly, is the Pym World?" In *The Life and Work of Barbara Pym*, edited by Dale Salwak, 50–57.

Baym, Nina. *Women's Fiction: A Guide to Novels By and About Women in America, 1820–1870*. Ithaca: Cornell University Press, 1978.

Beards, Virginia. "Margaret Drabble: Novels of a Cautionary Feminist." *Critique* 15 (1973): 35–47.

Bedient, Calvin. *Architects of the Self: George Eliot, D. H. Lawrence, and E. M. Forster*. Berkeley: University of California Press, 1972.

Beer, Patricia. *Reader, I Married Him: A Study of the Women Characters of Jane Austen, Charlotte Brontë, Elizabeth Gaskell, and George Eliot*. New York: Barnes and Noble, 1974.

Belkyn, Roslyn. "What George Eliot Knew: Women and Power in *Daniel Deronda*." *International Journal of Women's Studies* 4 (1981): 472–83.

Benet, Diana. *Something to Love: Barbara Pym's Novels*. Columbia: University of Missouri Press, 1986.

Bennett, Paula. *Family Relationships in the Novels of Jane Austen*. Ph.D. dissertation, University of Washington, 1980.

Bergonzi, Bernard. *The Situation of the Novel*. London: Macmillan, 1970.

Berke, Jacqueline, and Laura Berke. "Mothers and Daughters in *Wives and Daughters:* A Study of Gaskell's Last Novel." In *The Lost Tradition*, edited by Cathy N. Davidson and E. M. Broner, 95–109.

Bernikow, Louise. *Among Women*. New York: Harper, 1980.

Bersani, Leo. *A Future for Astyanax: Character and Desire in Literature*. New York: Columbia University Press, 1984.

Bettleheim, Bruno. *The Uses of Enchantment*. New York: Vintage, 1977.

Bick, Suzann. "Clouding the 'Severe Truth': Elizabeth Gaskell's Strategy in *The Life of Charlotte Brontë.*" *Essays in Arts and Sciences* 1 (1982): 33–47.

Blake, Kathleen. *Love and the Woman Question in Victorian Literature: The Art of Self-Postponement*. Totowa, N.J.: Barnes and Noble, 1983.

Bloom, Harold, ed. *Modern Critical Views: George Eliot*. New York: Chelsea House, 1986.

Brissenden, R. F. *"Mansfield Park:* Freedom and the Family." In *Jane Austen: Bicentenary Essays*, edited by John Halperin, 156–71.

Brooks, Peter. *Reading for the Plot: Design and Intention in Narrative*. New York: Knopf, 1984.

Brothers, Barbara. "Women Victimised by Fiction: Living and Loving in the Novels of Barbara Pym." In *Twentieth-Century Women Novelists*, edited by Thomas Staley, 61–80.

Brown, Carole D. "Dwindling into Life: A Jane Austen Heroine Grows Up." *International Journal of Women's Studies* 5 (1982): 460–69.

Brown, Julia Prewitt. *Jane Austen's Novels: Social Change and Literary Form*. Cambridge: Harvard University Press, 1979.

Brown, Lloyd W. "The Business of Marrying and Mothering." In *Jane Austen's Achievement: Papers Delivered at the Jane Austen Bicentennial Conference at the University of Alberta*, edited by Juliet McMaster, 27–43. New York: Barnes and Noble, 1976.

Brownstein, Rachel. *Becoming a Heroine*. New York: Penguin, 1984.

Buckley, Jerome H., ed. *The Worlds of Victorian Fiction*. Harvard English Studies, 6. Cambridge: Harvard University Press, 1975.

Burckhart, Charles. "Arnold Bennett and Margaret Drabble." In *Margaret Drabble*, edited by Dorey Schmidt, 91–103.

———. *The Pleasure of Miss Pym*. Austin: University of Texas Press, 1987.

Burstyn, Joan. *Victorian Education and the Ideal of Womanhood*. New Brunswick, N.J.: Rutgers University Press, 1984.

Butler, Marilyn. "The Uniqueness of Cynthia Kirkpatrick: Elizabeth Gaskell's *Wives and Daughters* and Maria Edgeworth's *Helen.*" *Review of English Studies* 23 (1972): 278–90.

Calder, Jenni. *Women and Marriage in Victorian Fiction*. New York: Oxford University Press, 1976.

Carroll, David. "*Middlemarch* and the Externality of Fact." In *This Particular Web: Essays on Middlemarch*, edited by Ian Adam, 73–90. Toronto: University of Toronto Press, 1975.

Carter, Angela. "The Language of Sisterhood." In *The State of the Language*, edited by Leonard Michaels and Christopher Ricks, 226–34.

Carter, Elizabeth A., and Monica McGoldrick, eds. *The Family Life Cycle: A Framework for Family Therapy.* New York: Gardner Press, 1980.

Cecil, David. *Victorian Novelists.* Chicago: University of Chicago Press, 1958.

Chase, Karen. *Eros and Psyche: The Representation of Personality in Charlotte Brontë, Charles Dickens and George Eliot.* New York: Methuen, 1984.

Cheung, King-Kok. "'Don't Tell': Imposed Silences in *The Color Purple* and *The Woman Warrior*." *PMLA* 103 (1988): 162–74.

Cixous, Hélène. "The Character of 'Character.'" Translated by Keith Cohen. *New Literary History* 5 (1974): 383–402.

Colby, Vineta. *Yesterday's Woman: Domestic Realism in the English Novel.* Princeton: Princeton University Press, 1974.

Coles, Robert. *Irony in the Mind's Eye: Essays on Novels by James Agee, Elizabeth Bowen, and George Eliot.* New York: New Directions, 1974.

Cooper-Clark, Diana. "Margaret Drabble: Cautious Feminist." *Atlantic Monthly* 246 (November 1980): 69–75.

Craik, W. A. *Elizabeth Gaskell and the English Provincial Novel.* London: Methuen, 1975.

Creighton, Joanne. "An Interview with Margaret Drabble." In *Margaret Drabble*, edited by Dorey Schmidt, 18–31.

——. *Margaret Drabble.* London: Methuen, 1985.

——. "Sisterly Symbiosis: Margaret Drabble's *The Waterfall* and A. S. Byatt's *The Game*." *Mosaic* 20, no. 1 (1987): 15–29.

Crosland, Margaret. *Beyond the Lighthouse: English Women Novelists in the Twentieth Century.* New York: Taplinger, 1981.

Cross, John. *George Eliot's Life.* 3 vols. New York: AMS Press, 1965.

Cunningham, Gail. "Women and Children First: The Novels of Margaret Drabble." In *Twentieth-Century Women Novelists*, edited by Thomas Staley, 130–52.

David, Deirdre. *Intellectual Women and the Victorian Patriarchy: Harriet Mill, Elizabeth Barrett Browning, George Eliot.* Ithaca: Cornell University Press, 1987.

Davidson, Arnold E. "Pride and Prejudice in Margaret Drabble's *A Summer Bird-Cage*." *Arizona Quarterly* 38 (1982): 303–10.

Davidson, Cathy N., and E. M. Broner, eds. *The Lost Tradition: Mothers and Daughters in Literature.* New York: Frederick Ungar, 1980.

Davidson, Donald. "What Metaphors Mean." In *On Metaphor*, edited by Sheldon Sacks, 29–45.

Dentith, Simon. *George Eliot.* Brighton, England: Harvester Press, 1986.

Derrida, Jacques. "White Mythology: Metaphor in the Text of Philosophy." In *Margins of Philosophy*, translated by Alan Bass, 207–71. Chicago: University of Chicago Press, 1982.

Dodsworth, Martin. "Women Without Men at Cranford." *Essays in Criticism* 13 (1963): 132–45.

Doheny, John. "George Eliot and Gwendolen Harleth." *Recovering Literature: A Journal of Contextualist Criticism* 5 (1976): 19–37.

Downing, Christine. *Psyche's Sisters: Reimagining the Meaning of Sisterhood.* New York: Harper, 1988.

Drabble, Margaret. "Gone But Not Quite Forgotten." *New York Times Book Review*, 25 July 1982.

————. "Novelists as Inspired Gossips." *MS,* April 1983, 32–33.

————. Personal interview with the author. New Orleans, La. 29 December 1988.

Du Plessis, Rachel Blau. "The Critique of Consciousness and Myth in Levertov, Rich and Rukeyser." In *Shakespeare's Sisters,* edited by Sandra M. Gilbert and Susan Gubar, 280–300. Bloomington: Indiana University Press, 1979.

————. "Psyche, or Wholeness." *Massachusette Review* 20 (1979): 77–96.

Duffy, Martha. "In Praise of Excellent Women." *Time,* 26 September 1983, 70.

Dundes, Alan. *Cinderella: A Casebook.* Madison: University of Wisconsin Press, 1988.

Dusinberre, Juliet. "A. S. Byatt." [Interview] In *Women Writers Talking,* edited by Janet M. Todd, 80–195.

Duthie, Enid L. *The Themes of Elizabeth Gaskell.* Totowa, N.J.: Rowman and Littlefield, 1980.

Easson, Angus. "Domestic Romanticism: Elizabeth Gaskell and *The Life of Charlotte Brontë." Durham University Journal* 73 (1981): 168–76.

————. *Elizabeth Gaskell.* London: Routledge and Kegan Paul, 1979.

Echols, Alice. *Daring to Be Bad: Radical Feminism in America, 1967–1975.* Minneapolis: University of Minnesota Press, 1989.

Edwards, Lee R. "Jerusalem the Golden: A Fable for Our Time." *Women's Studies* 6 (1979): 321–34.

————. "The Labors of Psyche: Toward a Theory of Female Heroism." *Critical Inquiry* 6 (1979): 33–49.

————. *Psyche as Hero: Female Heroism and Fictional Form.* Middletown, Conn.: Wesleyan University Press, 1984.

————. "Women, Energy, and *Middlemarch." In Middlemarch,* by George Eliot, edited by Bert G. Hornback, 683–93.

Efrig, Gail. "The Middle Ground." In *Margaret Drabble,* edited by Dorey Schmidt, 178–85.

Eichenbaum, Luise, and Susie Orbach. *Between Women: Love, Envy, and Competition in Women's Friendships.* New York: Viking, 1988.

Eliot, George. *Essays of George Eliot.* Edited by Thomas Pinney. New York: Columbia University Press, 1963.

Emery, Laura Comer. *George Eliot's Creative Conflict: The Other Side of Silence.* Berkeley: University of California Press, 1976.

Ezell, Margaret. " 'What Shall We Do With Our Old Maids?': Barbara Pym and the 'Woman Question.' " *International Journal of Women's Studies* 7 (1984): 450–65.

Fair, Thomas P. "The Paternal Model in the Novels of Elizabeth Gaskell." Ph.D. dissertation, University of Colorado, 1986.

The Female Aegis, or, The Duties of Women. Edited by Gina Luria. New York: Garland, 1974.

Fergus, Jan S. "Sex and Social Life in Jane Austen's Novels." In *Jane Austen in a Social Context,* edited by David Monaghan, 66–68.

Ferguson, Frances. "The Unfamiliarity of Familiar Letters." In *The State of the Language,* edited by Leonard Michaels and Christopher Ricks, 78–88.

Ferguson, Mary Anne. "The Female Novel of Development and the Myth of Psyche." In *The Voyage In,* edited by Elizabeth Abel et al., 228–43.

Ffrench, Yvonne. *Mrs. Gaskell.* Denver: Alan Swallow, 1949.

Firchow, Peter. "Margaret Drabble." [Interview] In *The Writer's Place: Interviews on the Literary Situation in Contemporary Britain*, edited by Peter Firchow, 102–21. Minneapolis: University of Minnesota Press, 1975.

———. "Rosamond's Complaint: Margaret Drabble's *The Millstone* (1966)." In *Old Lines, New Forces: Essays on the Contemporary British Novel, 1960–1970*, edited by Robert K. Morris, 93–108. Rutherford, N.J.: Fairleigh Dickinson University Press, 1976.

Fishel, Elizabeth. *Sisters*. New York: William Morrow, 1979.

Ford, George Henry, ed. *Victorian Fiction: A Second Guide to Research*. New York: Modern Language Association, 1978.

Foster, Shirley. *Victorian Women's Fiction: Marriage, Freedom, and the Individual*. London: Croom, Helm, 1985.

Foster, Thomas. "History, Critical Theory, and Women's Social Practices: 'Women's Time' and *Housekeeping*." *Signs* 14 (1988): 73–99.

Fox-Genovese, Elizabeth. "The Ambiguities of Female Identity: A Reading of the Novels of Margaret Drabble." *Partisan Review* 46 (1979): 234–61.

Freadman, Richard. *Eliot, James and The Fictional Self*. London: Macmillan, 1986.

Fulmer, Constance Marie. "Contrasting Pairs of Heroines in George Eliot's Fiction." *Studies in the Novel* 6 (1974): 288–94.

———. *George Eliot: A Reference Guide*. Boston: G. K. Hall, 1977.

Gallop, Jane. *The Daughter's Seduction: Feminism and Psychoanalysis*. Ithaca: Cornell University Press, 1982.

Ganz, Margaret. *Elizbeth Gaskell: The Artist in Conflict*. New York: Twayne, 1969.

Gaskell, Elizabeth. *The Letters of Mrs. Gaskell*. Edited by J. A. V. Chapple and Arthur Pollard. Cambridge: Harvard University Press, 1967.

———. *The Life of Charlotte Brontë*. New York: Penguin, 1975.

Gardiner, Judith Kegan. "On Female Identity and Writing by Women." *Critical Inquiry* 8 (1981): 347–61.

Gérin, Winifred. *Elizabeth Gaskell: A Biography*. Oxford: Oxford University Press, 1976.

Gilbert, Sandra M., and Susan Gubar. *The Madwoman in the Attic: The Woman Writer and the Nineteenth-Century Literary Imagination*. New Haven: Yale University Press, 1979.

———. *The War of the Words*. Vol. 1 of *No Man's Land: The Place of the Woman Writer in the Twentieth Century*. New Haven: Yale University Press, 1988.

Gilligan, Carol. *In A Different Voice: Psychological Theory and Women's Development*. Cambridge: Harvard University Press, 1982.

Gisborne, Thomas M. A. *An Enquiry into the Duties of the Female Sex*. Edited by Gina Luria. New York: Garland, 1974.

Gorer, Geoffrey. "Poor Honey: Some Notes on Jane Austen and Her Mother." *London Magazine* 4 (1957): 35–48.

Gornick, Vivian. "The World of Our Mothers." *The New York Times Book Review*, 22 November 1987.

Gorsky, Susan R. "Old Maids and New Women: Alternatives to Marriage in Women's Novels, 1847–1915." *Journal of Popular Culture* 7 (1973): 68–85.

Green, Harvey. *The Light of Home: An Intimate View of the Lives of Women in Victorian America*. New York: Pantheon, 1983.

Grimm, Jacob, and Wilhelm Grimm. *Grimm's Fairy Tales*. Translated by E. V. Lucas, Lucy Crane, and Marian Edwards. New York: Grosset and Dunlap, 1946.

Haffenden, John, ed. *Novelists in Interview*. New York: Methuen, 1985.

Haight, Gordon. *George Eliot: A Biography*. New York: Oxford University Press, 1968.

Haight, Gordon, and Rosemary T. Van Ardsel, eds. *George Eliot: A Centenary Tribute*. London: Macmillan, 1982.

Hagstrum, Jean H. "Eros and Psyche: Some Versions of Romantic Love and Delicacy." *Critical Inquiry* 3 (1977): 521–42.

Halperin, John. "Barbara Pym and the War of the Sexes." In *The Life and Work of Barbara Pym*, edited by Dale Salwak, 88–100.

———. *Egoism and Self-Discovery in the Victorian Novel*. New York: Burt Franklin, 1974.

———, ed. *Jane Austen: Bicentenary Essays*. New York: Cambridge University Press, 1975.

Hardin, Nancy S. "Drabble's *The Millstone*: A Fable for Our Times." *Critique* 15 (1973): 22–34.

———. "An Interview with Margaret Drabble." *Contemporary Literature* 14 (1973): 273–95.

Hardy, Barbara. "Implications and Incompleteness: George Eliot's *Middlemarch*." In *The Victorian Novel: Essays in Criticism*, edited by Ian Watt, 289–323. New York: Oxford University Press, 1971.

———. "The Moment of Disenchantment." In *Modern Critical Views*, edited by Harold Bloom, 45–54.

Harvey, W. J. *The Art of George Eliot*. London: Chatto and Windus, 1963.

———. *Character and the Novel*. Ithaca: Cornell University Press, 1965.

Hegel, George W. F. *The Phenomenology of the Mind*. Translated and introduced by J. B. Baillie. New York: Harper, 1967.

Heilbrun, Carolyn. *Reinventing Womanhood*. New York: Norton, 1979.

Highbie, Robert. *Character and Structure in the English Novel*. Gainesville: University of Florida Press, 1984.

Hirsch, Marianne. "Spiritual Bildung: The Beautiful Soul as Paradigm." In *The Voyage In*, edited by Elizabeth Abel et al., 23–48.

Hochman, Baruch. *Character in Literature*. Ithaca: Cornell University Press, 1985.

———. *The Test of Character*. Rutherford, N.J.: Fairleigh Dickinson University Press, 1983.

Hollander, Anne. *Seeing Through Clothes*. New York: Avon, 1980.

Homans, Margaret. "Eliot, Wordsworth, and the Scenes of the Sisters' Instruction." *Critical Inquiry* 8 (1981): 223–41.

Hopkins, Annette B. *Elizabeth Gaskell: Her Life and Work*. New York: Farrar, Straus, and Giroux, 1971.

———. "Letter of Advice." *London Magazine* 1 (1954): 73–75.

Hudson, Glenda Ann. "Sibling Relationships in Jane Austen's Fiction." Ph.D. dissertation, Vanderbilt University, 1987.

Hunt, Linda. "Charlotte Brontë and the Suffering Sisterhood." *Colby Library Quarterly* 19, no. 1 (1983): 7–17.

Hutcheson, John. "Subdued Feminism: Jane Austen, Charlotte Brontë, and George Eliot." *International Journal of Women's Studies* 6 (1983): 230–57.

Ibsen, Charles A., and Patricia Klobus. "Fictive Kin Term Use and Social Relationships: Alternative Interpretations." *Journal of Marriage and the Family* 34 (1972): 615–20.

Janeway, Elizabeth. *Between Myth and Morning: Women Awakening*. New York: William Morrow, 1975.

Jones, R. T. *George Eliot*. Cambridge, England: Cambridge University Press, 1970.

Juhasz, Suzanne. "Facilitating Environments." Unpublished manuscript, 1989.

———. "Reading Jane Austen's Letters." Unpublished essay, 1983.

Kapp, Isa. "Out of the Swim with Barbara Pym." *American Scholar* 52 (1983): 237–42.

Kaye-Smith, Sheila. "Four and Twenty Families." In *More About Jane Austen*, edited by Sheila Kaye-Smith and G. B. Stern, 120–40. New York: Harper, 1949.

Keats, John. "Ode to Psyche." In *Complete Poems and Selected Letters*, edited by Clarence DeWitt Thorpe, 343–4. New York: Doubleday, 1935.

Keener, Frederick M. "Barbara Pym Herself and Jane Austen." *Twentieth-Century Literature* 31 (1985): 89–110.

Kennard, Jean E. *Victims of Convention*. Hamden, Conn.: Archon, 1978.

Keyser, Elizabeth Lennox. "Alcott's Portraits of the Artist as Little Woman." *International Journal of Women's Studies* 5 (1982): 445–59.

Kiely, Robert. "The Limits of Dialogue in *Middlemarch*." In *The Worlds of Victorian Fiction*, edited by Jerome Buckley, 103–24.

Kirkham, Margaret. *Jane Austen, Feminism and Fiction*. Totowa, N.J.: Barnes and Noble, 1983.

Kohut, Heinz. *How Does Analysis Cure?* Edited by Arnold Goldberg. Chicago: University of Chicago Press, 1984.

Kucich, John. *Repression in Victorian Fiction: Charlotte Brontë, George Eliot, and Charles Dickens*. Berkeley: University of California Press, 1987.

Lansbury, Coral. *Elizabeth Gaskell: The Novel of Social Crisis*. London: Paul Elek, 1975.

———. *Elizabeth Gaskell*. Boston: Twayne, 1984.

Lanser, Susan. "No Connections Subsequent: Jane Austen's World of Sisterhood." In *The Sister Bond*, edited by Toni A. H. McNaron, 51–67.

Larson, Edith. "The Celebration of the Ordinary in Barbara Pym's Novels." *San Jose Studies* 9, no. 2 (1983): 17–22.

Lasser, Carol. " 'Let Us Be Sisters Forever': The Sororal Model of Nineteenth-Century Female Friendship." *Signs* 14 (1988): 158–81.

Leavis, F. R. *The Great Tradition*. New York: New York University Press, 1963.

Lenta, Margaret. "Jane Austen's Feminism: An Original Response to Convention." *Critical Quarterly* 23, no. 3 (1981): 27–36.

Leonard, Linda. *The Wounded Woman: Healing the Father-Daughter Relationship*. Boulder, Colo.: Shambhala Press, 1983.

Levine, George. *The Realistic Imagination: English Fiction from* Frankenstein *to* Lady Chatterley. Chicago: University of Chicago Press, 1981.

Liddell, Robert. *The Novels of George Eliot*. New York: St. Martin's Press, 1977.

————. *The Novels of Jane Austen*. London: Longmans, 1963.

Lively, Penelope. "The World of Barbara Pym." In *The Life and Work of Barbara Pym*, edited by Dale Salwak, 45–49.

Long, Robert Emmet. *Barbara Pym*. New York: Ungar, 1986.

MacDonald. Susan Peck. "Jane Austen and the Tradition of the Absent Mother." In *The Lost Tradition*, edited by Cathy N. Davidson and E. M. Broner, 58–69.

Manheimer, Joan. "Margaret Drabble and the Journey to the Self." *Studies in the Literary Imagination* 11 (1978): 127–43.

Mann, Karen B. *The Language That Makes George Eliot's Fiction*. Baltimore: Johns Hopkins University Press, 1983.

Margolies, Eva. *The Best of Friends, The Worst of Enemies*. New York: Doubleday, 1985.

Marks, Elaine, and Isabelle de Courtivron, eds. *New French Feminisms*. New York: Schocken, 1981.

Martin, Carol A. "No Angel in the House: Victorian Mothers and Daughters in George Eliot and Elizabeth Gaskell." *Midwest Quarterly* 24 (1983): 297–314.

Martin, Hazel T. *Petticoat Rebels: A Study of the Novels of Social Protest of George Eliot, Elizabeth Gaskell and Charlotte Brontë*. New York: Helios, 1968.

May, Gita. "Concluding Remarks." In *The Poetics of Gender*, edited by Nancy K. Miller, 297–99.

McCarthy, Fiona. "The Drabble Sisters." *The Guardian*. 13 April 1967, 8.

McNaron, Toni A. H. "How Little We Know and How Much We Feel." In *The Sister Bond*, edited by Toni A. H. McNaron, 1–10.

————, ed. *The Sister Bond: A Feminist View of a Timeless Connection*. New York: Pergamon, 1985.

Michaels, Leonard, and Christopher Ricks, eds. *The State of the Language*. Berkeley: University of California Press, 1980.

Michie, Helena. "The Battle for Sisterhood: Christina Rossetti's Strategies for Control in her Sister Poems." *Journal of Pre-Raphaelite Studies* 3, no. 2 (1983): 38–55.

————. "Mother, Sister, Other: The 'Other' Woman in Feminist Theory." *Literature and Psychology* 32, no. 4 (1986): 1–10.

"*Middlemarch*." In *Middlemarch*, by George Eliot, edited by Bert G. Hornback, 645–48.

Miles, Rosalind. *The Female Form: Women Writers and the Conquest of the Novel*. New York: Routledge and Kegan Paul, 1987.

Miller, D. A. *Narrative and its Discontents: Problems of Closure in the Traditional Novel*. Princeton: Princeton University Press, 1981.

Miller, J. Hillis. *Fiction and Repetition: Seven English Novels*. Cambridge: Harvard University Press, 1982.

————. *The Form of Victorian Fiction*. Notre Dame, Ind.: Notre Dame University Press, 1968.

————. "Optic and Semiotic in *Middlemarch*." In *The Worlds of Victorian Fiction*, edited by Jerome Buckley, 125–45.

Miller, Nancy K. *Subject to Change: Reading Feminist Writing*. New York: Columbia University Press, 1988.

————, ed. *The Poetics of Gender*. New York: Columbia University Press, 1986.

Milton, Barbara. "The Art of Fiction LXX." [Interview with Margaret Drabble] *Paris Review* 20, no. 74 (1978): 40–65.

Mitchell, Juliet. *Psychoanalysis and Feminism.* New York: Random House, 1974.

Moers, Ellen. *Literary Women.* Garden City, N.Y.: Doubleday, 1976.

Moler, Kenneth. *Jane Austen's Art of Allusion.* Lincoln: University of Nebraska Press, 1969.

Monaghan, David. *Jane Austen: Structure and Social Vision.* New York: Barnes and Noble, 1980.

———, ed. *Jane Austen in a Social Context.* New York: Barnes and Noble, 1981.

Moran, Mary Hurley. *Margaret Drabble: Existing Within Structures.* Carbondale: Southern Illinois University Press, 1983.

Morgan, Susan. "Polite Lies: The Veiled Heroine of *Sense and Sensibility.*" *Nineteenth-Century Fiction* 31 (1976): 188–205.

Myer, Valerie Grosvenor. *Margaret Drabble: Puritanism and Permissiveness.* London: Vision Press, 1974.

Nardin, Jane. *Barbara Pym.* Boston: Twayne, 1985.

———. *Those Elegant Decorums: The Concept of Propriety in Jane Austen's Novels.* Albany: State University of New York Press, 1973.

Naumann, Walter. "The Architecture of George Eliot's Novels." *Modern Language Quarterly* 9 (1948): 34–50.

Nestor, Pauline. *Female Friendships and Communities.* Oxford: Clarendon Press, 1985.

Neumann, Erich. *Amor and Psyche: The Psychic Development of the Feminine. A Commentary on the Tale by Apuleius.* Translated by Ralph Manheim. Bollingen Series, 54. Princeton: Princeton University Press, 1971.

Newton, Judith Lowder. *Women, Power, and Subversion.* Athens: University of Georgia Press, 1981.

Norton, Charles Eliot. *The Letters of Charles Eliot Norton.* Cambridge, Mass.: The Riverside Press, 1913.

Nystul, Nancy. "*Daniel Deronda:* A Family Romance." *Enclitic* 7 (1983): 45–53.

Olsen, Tillie. *Silences.* New York: Delacorte, 1978.

Paris, Bernard. *Character and Conflict in Jane Austen's Novels: A Psychological Approach.* Detroit: Wayne State University Press, 1978.

Parker, Gillian, and Janet Todd. "Margaret Drabble." [Interview] In *Women Writers Talking,* edited by Janet Todd, 160–78.

Patterson, Emily H. "Family and Pilgrimage Themes in *Mansfield Park.*" *College Language Association Journal* 20 (1976): 14–18.

Pearson, Carol, and Katherine Pope. *The Female Hero in American and British Literature.* New York: R. R. Bowker, 1981.

Poland, Nancy. "Margaret Drabble: 'There Must be a Lot of People Like Me.'" *Midwest Quarterly* 16 (1975): 255–67.

Pollard, Arthur. *Mrs. Gaskell: Novelist and Biographer.* Cambridge: Harvard University Press, 1966.

Preussner, Dee. "Talking with Margaret Drabble." *Modern Fiction Studies* 25 (1979–80): 563–77.

Price, Martin. "The Nature of Decision." In *Modern Critical Views,* edited by Harold Bloom, 223–42.

Putzell-Korab, Sara M., and Martha Watson Brownley. "Dorothea and Her Husbands: Some Autobiographical Sources for Speculation." *Victorian Newsletter* 68 (1985): 15–19.

Pym, Barbara. *A Very Private Eye: An Autobiography in Diaries and Letters*. Edited by Hazel Holt and Hilary Pym. New York: Dutton, 1984.

Rayson, Ann. "Motherhood in the Novels of Margaret Drabble." *Frontiers* 3, no. 2 (1978): 43–46.

Redinger, Ruby. *George Eliot: The Emergent Self*. New York: Knopf, 1975.

"Reputations Revisited." *Times Literary Supplement*, 21 January 1977, 66–68.

Rich, Adrienne. *On Lies, Secrets, and Silence: Selected Prose 1966–1979*. New York: Norton, 1979.

———. *Snapshots of a Daughter-in-Law: Poems 1954–1962*. New York: Norton, 1967.

Ricoeur, Paul. "The Metaphorical Process as Cognition, Imagination, and Feeling." In *On Metaphor*, edited by Sheldon Sacks, 141–57.

Robinson, Lillian. *Sex, Class and Culture*. Bloomington: Indiana University Press, 1978.

Rose, Ellen C. "Margaret Drabble: Surviving the Future." *Critique* 15 (1973): 4–21.

———. *The Novels of Margaret Drabble: Equivocal Figures*. Totowa, N.J.: Barnes and Noble, 1980.

Rossen, Janice. *The World of Barbara Pym*. New York: St. Martin's Press, 1987.

Rossetti, Christina. "Goblin Market." In *Poems*, 1–20. London: Macmillan, 1891.

Roth, Barry, and Joel Weinsteimer. *An Annotated Bibliography of Jane Austen Studies 1952–1972*. Charlottesville: University of Virginia Press, 1973.

Rotner, Arnold Herbert. "Mrs. Gaskell's Art." Ph.D. dissertation, University of Colorado, 1967.

Rowse, A. L. "Miss P and Miss A." In *The Life and Work of Barbara Pym*, edited by Dale Salwak, 64–71.

Roxman, Susanna. *Guilt and Glory: Studies in Margaret Drabble's Novels, 1963–1980*. Stockholm: Almquist and Wiksell, 1984.

Rubenius, Aina. *The Woman Question in Mrs. Gaskell's Life and Works*. New York: Russell and Russell, 1950.

Rubenstein, Roberta. "*The Waterfall:* The Myth of Psyche, Romantic Tradition, and the Female Quest." In *Margaret Drabble*, edited by Dorey Schmidt, 139–57.

Ruoff, Gene W. "Anne Elliott's Dowry: Reflections on the Ending of *Persusasion*." *Wordsworth Circle* 7 (1976): 342–51.

Sacks, Sheldon, ed. *On Metaphor*. Chicago: University of Chicago Press, 1979.

Sadler, Lynn Veach. *Margaret Drabble*. Boston: Twayne, 1986.

Sadoff, Diane. *Monsters of Affection: Dickens, Eliot and Brontë on Fatherhood*. Baltimore: Johns Hopkins University Press, 1982.

Sage, Lorna. "Female Fictions: The Women Novelists." In *The Contemporary English Novel*, edited by Malcolm Bradbury and David Palmer, 67–88. Stratford-upon-Avon Studies, 18. New York: Holmes and Meier, 1979.

Salwak, Dale, ed. *The Life and Work of Barbara Pym*. London: Macmillan, 1987.

Schmidt, Dorey, ed. *Margaret Drabble: Golden Realms*. Living Author Series, 4. Edinburg, Texas: Pan American University Press, 1982.

Schor, Naomi. "Reading Double: Sand's Difference." In *The Poetics of Gender*, edited by Nancy K. Miller, 248–69.

Sexton, Anne. *Transformations*. Boston: Houghton Mifflin, 1971.

Shapiro, Anna. "The Resurrection of Barbara Pym." *Saturday Review*, July-August 1983, 29–31.

Sharp, Ronald A. *Friendship and Literature: Spirit and Form*. Durham, N.C.: Duke University Press, 1986.

Shelston, Alan. Introduction to *The Life of Charlotte Brontë*, by Elizabeth Gaskell. New York: Penguin, 1975.

Sherwood, Rhonda Irene. "'A Special Kind of Double': Sisters in British and American Fiction." Ph.D. dissertation, University of Wisconsin–Milwaukee, 1987.

Short, Clarice. "Studies in Gentleness." *Western Humanities Review* 11 (1957): 387–93.

Showalter, Elaine. *A Literature of Their Own: British Women Novelists from Brontë to Lessing*. Princeton: Princeton University Press, 1977.

———, ed. *The New Feminist Criticism: Essays on Women, Literature and Theory*. New York: Pantheon, 1985.

Siefert Susan. *The Dilemma of the Talented Heroine: A Study in Nineteenth-Century Fiction*. Montreal: Eden, 1977.

Sinclair, May. *The Three Brontës*. New York: Kennicat Press, 1967.

Smith-Rosenberg, Carroll. "The Female World of Love and Ritual." In *A Heritage of Her Own*, edited by Nancy F. Cott and Elizabeth H. Peck, 311–42. New York: Simon and Schuster, 1979.

Sophocles. *Antigone*. In *The Theban Plays*, translated by E. F. Watling, 126–62. Harmondsworth, England: Penguin, 1972.

Southam, B. C., ed. *Jane Austen: The Critical Heritage*. London: Routledge and Kegan Paul, 1968.

Spacks, Patricia Meyer. *The Adolescent Idea: Myths of Youth and the Adult Imagination*. New York: Harper, 1981.

———. *The Female Imagination*. New York: Knopf, 1975.

———. Introduction to *Contemporary Women Novelists*, edited by Patricia Meyer Spacks. Englewood Cliffs, N.J.: Prentice Hall, 1977.

———. "Muted Discord: Generational Conflict in Jane Austen." In *Jane Austen in a Social Context*, edited by David Monaghan, 159–79.

———. "Sisters." In *Fetter'd or Free? British Women Novelists, 1670–1815*, edited by Mary Anne Schofield and Cecelia Macheski, 136–51. Athens: Ohio University Press, 1986.

———. "Taking Care: Some Women Novelists." *Novel* 6 (1972): 36–51.

Spivak, Gayatri Chakravorty. "Three Feminist Readings: McCullers, Drabble, Habermas." *Union Seminary Quarterly Review* 35 (1979–80): 15–34.

Staley, Thomas. Introduction to *Twentieth-Century Women Novelists*, edited by Thomas Staley.

———, ed. *Twentieth-Century Women Novelists*. Totowa, N.J.: Barnes and Noble, 1982.

Stoneman, Patsy. *Elizabeth Gaskell*. Bloomington: Indiana University Press, 1987.

Suleiman, Susan Rubin. "On Maternal Splitting: A Propos of Mary Gordon's *Men and Angels*." *Signs* 14 (1988): 25–41.

Sulloway, Alison G. *Jane Austen and the Province of Womanhood*. Philadelphia: University of Pennsylvania Press, 1989.

Tanner, Tony. *Adultery in the Novel: Contract and Transgression*. Baltimore: Johns Hopkins Press, 1979.

———. *Jane Austen*. Cambridge: Harvard University Press, 1986.

Tarratt, Margaret. "Cranford and 'The Strict Code of Gentility.'" *Essays in Criticism* 18 (1968): 152–63.

Taylor, Ina. *Victorian Sisters*. London: Weidenfield and Nicolson, 1987.

Thomas, Jeannie. *Reading* Middlemarch: *Reclaiming the Middle Distance*. Ann Arbor: University of Michigan Research Press, 1988.

Todd, Janet M. *Women's Friendship in Literature*. New York: Columbia University Press, 1980.

———, ed. *Women Writers Talking*. New York: Holmes and Meier, 1983.

Twitchell, James. *Forbidden Partners: The Incest Taboo in Modern Culture*. New York: Columbia University Press, 1982.

Uglow, Jennifer. *George Eliot*. New York: Random House, 1987.

Ulanov, Ann, and Barry Ulanov. *Cinderella and Her Sisters: The Envied and the Envying*. Philadelphia: Westminster Press, 1983.

Van Boheemen, Christine. *The Novel as Family Romance: Language, Gender and Authority from Fielding to Joyce*. Ithaca: Cornell University Press, 1987.

Veblen, Thorstein. *The Theory of the Leisure Class*. New York: New American Library, 1953.

Vicinus, Martha, ed. *Suffer and Be Still*. Bloomington: Indiana University Press, 1973.

———, ed. *A Widening Sphere*. Bloomington: Indiana University Press, 1977.

Viner, Alexander E. S. *George Eliot*. London: Oliver and Boyd, 1971.

Wallace, Marjorie. *The Silent Twins*. New York: Ballantine, 1986.

Warhol, Robyn R. "Toward a Theory of the Engaging Narrator: Earnest Interventions in Gaskell, Stowe, and Eliot." *PMLA* 101 (1986): 811–18.

Watson, Barbara Bellow. "On Power and the Literary Text." *Signs* 1 (1975): 111–18.

Welch, James. *Elizabeth Gaskell: An Annotated Bibliography, 1929–1975*. New York: Garland, 1977.

Weldon, Fay. *Letters to Alice: On First Reading Jane Austen*. New York: Taplinger, 1985.

Wherritt, T. Mildred. "For Better or for Worse: Marriage Proposals in Jane Austen's Novels." *Midwest Quarterly* 17 (1976): 229–49.

White, Marjorie Taggart, and Marcella Baker Weiner. *The Theory and Practice of Self Psychology*. New York: Brunner-Mazel, 1986.

Williams, Merryn. *Women in the English Novel, 1800–1900*. New York: St. Martin's Press, 1984.

Williams, Pat. "The Sisters Drabble." *Sunday Times Magazine*, 6 August 1967, 12–15.

Wollstonecraft, Mary. *Thoughts on the Education of Daughters, with Reflections on Female Conduct, in the More Important Duties of Life*. Edited by Gina Luria. New York: Garland, 1974.

Woolf, Virginia. *The Common Reader*. First Series. New York: Harcourt Brace, 1953.

———. *A Room of One's Own*. New York: Harcourt, 1929.

Wright, Edgar. *Mrs. Gaskell: The Basis for Reassessment*. New York: Oxford University Press, 1965.

Zimmerman, Bonnie. "Gwendolen Harleth and 'The Girl of the Period,'" In *George Eliot: Centenary Essays and an Unpublished Fragment*, edited by Anne Smith, 196–219. London: Vision, 1980.

———. " 'Radiant as a Diamond': George Eliot, Jewelry, and the Female Role." *Criticism* 19 (1977): 212–22.

Zipes, Jack. *The Brothers Grimm: From Enchanted Forests to the Modern World*. New York: Routledge, 1988.

Index

Adultery, 20, 96
After Julius (Howard): 30, 94, 108–11;
  conclusion of, 110; individuation in,
  108; role of father in, 110; role rever-
  sals in, 109; sisters as opposites in, 108
Alcott, Louisa May: *Little Women*, 13, 29
Antigone, 16, 21, 24
Aphrodite, 23
Atkins, Dale: *Sisters*, 14, 19–20
Auerbach, Nina: *Communities of Women*,
  15, 22, 35, 60, 62–63, 72, 76–77, 81;
  Woman and the Demon, 73
Aunts, 27–28, 29, 56, 80, 121
Austen, Cassandra, 33
Austen, Jane: 29, 33–53; *Emma*, 26, 29,
  34, 50–52; juvenilia, 34; *Lesley Castle*,
  34–35; *Mansfield Park*, 26, 29, 34, 39,
  49–50, 82; *Northanger Abbey*, 34; *Per-
  suasion*, 29, 34, 45–49; *Pride and Preju-
  dice*, 13, 20, 25, 26, 29, 34, 39–45, 79;
  Sanditon, 34; *Sense and Sensibility*, 26,
  29, 34, 35–39; *The Three Sisters* 34, 35;
  The Watsons, 34. *See also* specific works

Bad Sister, The (Tennant): aunts in, 123;
  identity in, 124, 125, 126; narrator in,
  122, 124; revision of other works, 122,
  123, 124; role splitting in, 31, 125;
  sisterhood in, 120; sisters' relation-
  ships in, 31, 120, 123, 124, 126; sur-
  realism in, 31, 124
Bank, Stephen, and Michael Kahn, 36,
  40
Basch, Françoise, 43
"Beauty and the Beast," 21–22
Beer, Patricia, 35, 85
Benet, Diana, 100, 107
Bernikow, Louise: *Among Women*, 14, 17,
  18
Bersani, Leo, 49
Bettleheim, Bruno, 22
Bick, Suzann, 73

Biography, 70–71
Brissenden, R. F., 50
Brontë, Anne, 73; and Emily, twinship
  transference, 73, 134
Brontë, Branwell, 73, 75
Brontë, Charlotte: in *Cranford*, 76–77;
  Jane Eyre, 28; *Shirley*, 28; *Villette*, 28.
  See also *Life of Charlotte Brontë, The*
Brontë, Emily, 70–72, 74; and Anne,
  twinship transference, 73, 134
Brontë, Patrick, 71
Brothers: brother-lover, 50, 75, 90, 95,
  106–7, 108; of sisters, 24, 50, 57, 58,
  61, 67, 80
Brownstein, Rachel, 44
Butler, Samuel, 35
Byatt, A. S. (sister to Margaret Drabble):
  The Game, 111; *Still Life*, 13, 111

Calder, Jenni, 80
Cecil, David, 55
"Cinderella," 13, 21, 23–34, 30, 45, 97,
  126; *The Bad Sister* as version of, 123
Cixous, Hélène, 21
Clarke, Chrissey (sister to George Eliot),
  78
Class, division by marriage, 27, 29, 38,
  50
Clothing, 27, 97, 105, 106, 114, 117; in
  characterization, 85–86, 103–4
Collins, Wilkie: *No Name*, 13, 29;
  Woman in White, 13, 29
Communication, 37, 38, 44, 51, 97; dou-
  ble messages, 41; silences, 16, 38, 44–
  45, 48–49
Complementarity, 56, 100, 115–16
Conclusions, of novels, 27, 31, 45, 110,
  118, 125, 126. *See also* specific titles
Cranford (Gaskell): brother and father in,
  58, 61; conclusion of, 61, 62; Deborah
  in, 57–62; repression in, 57–60; role
  splitting, 60; sisterhood, 60, 62

Creighton, Joanne, 15, 97–98, 111–12, 115
Cunningham, Gail, 95

Daniel Deronda (Eliot): conclusion of, 92; half sisters in, 89; role splitting in, 90; sister plot, 90
Davidson, Arnold, 112
Derrida, Jacques, 15, 31
Dodsworth, Martin, 59, 60
Downing, Christine: *Psyche's Sisters*, 14, 16, 31
Drabble, Margaret, 97, 111–17. See also *Summer Bird-Cage, A*

Easson, Angus, 64–65
Edwards, Lee, 85
Eichenbaum, Luise, 19, 119
Eliot, George: 30, 78–93; compared to Gaskell, 79; *Daniel Deronda*, 30, 78, 89–92; *Middlemarch*, 24, 25–26, 30, 78, 83–89; *The Mill on the Floss*, 30, 78, 80–83; portrayal of sisters in, 78, 79, 91, 92. *See also* specific titles
Emma (Jane Austen): communication in, 51; conclusion of, 52; father in, 50–51; role splitting in, 51; sisterhood in, 52
Ezell, Margaret, 95

Fairy tales, 45; polarization in, 22; three brothers motif, 22. *See also* "Beauty and the Beast," "Cinderella," and "Snow White and Rose Red"
Fathers, 45, 46–47, 58, 107, 123; daughters aligned with, 26, 42, 50–51, 52, 63–64, 65
Feminist criticism, 102
Ffrench, Yvonne, 76
Fishel, Elizabeth: *Sisters*, 14, 16, 22, 42
Fox-Genovese, Elizabeth, 117
Freud, Sigmund: Oedipal stage, 17, 23–24; separation, 17
Friend-sisters, 14, 19, 30, 60

Gallop, Jane, 17, 125
Gaskell, Elizabeth: 29, 54–77; *Cranford*, 25, 26, 27, 29, 30, 54, 55, 57–63; *The Life of Charlotte Brontë*, 29, 30, 54, 55, 70–77; *Mary Barton*, 29–30, 55–56; "Mr. Harrison's Confessions," 56–57; *Wives and Daughters*, 13, 26, 29, 54, 55, 63–70. *See also* specific titles

Gilbert, Sandra, and Susan Gubar, 28, 96
Gissing, George, 29
Godwin, Gail: *Mother and Two Daughters* 14, 120; *Odd Woman*, 14, 29, 120
Gorer, Geoffrey, 33
Gubar, Susan, and Sandra Gilbert, 28, 96

Hegel, 16, 24
Heilbrun, Carolyn, 23
Highbie, Robert, 21
Hirsch, Marianne, 24
Holden, Ursula: *Wider Pools*, 120
Homosexuality, 120–21
Howard, Elizabeth Jane, 30, 94, 108–11
Hudson, Glenda Ann, 15, 33, 44

Incest: brother-sister, 27, 50, 58; father-daughter, 26, 43, 64–65, 69
Interchangeability, of sisters, 38, 44, 47, 48
Intertextuality, 97, 103

Juhasz, Suzanne, 37

Kahn, Michael, and Stephen Bank, 36, 40
King Lear, 22, 24

Lansbury, Coral, 55, 65, 74
Lanser, Susan, 14, 19, 33, 47
Lasser, Carol, 14
Lesbianism. *See* Homosexuality
Lesley Castle (Jane Austen), 34–35
Letters, 71
Life of Charlotte Brontë, The (Gaskell): Brontë juvenilia, 72; conclusion of, 76; Charlotte and her sisters, 70, 72–73; family, 73; father in, 71, 72; Gaskell in, 92–93; repression, 72, 74; role splitting, 75; suppression of anger, 74
Long, Robert, 95, 98

Mansfield Park (Jane Austen): aunts in, 28; conclusion of, 50
Marriage Plot, 27, 29; in Austen, 34, 38, 39, 44, 47, 53; in Gaskell, 54, 56, 61, 63, 76; in twentieth-century works, 97
Marriage Proposals, 48, 50, 99, 100
Mary Barton (Gaskell): aunts in, 28, 56; conclusion of, 56; repression in, 56
Martineau, Harriet: *Deerbrook*, 28
McNaron, Toni: *Sister Bond*, 14

Metaphors, 15–16, 30
Michie, Helena, 118
Middlemarch (Eliot): Dorothea Brooke, 87; identity in, 89; polarization in, 85, 86; role splitting, 87–88, 89; sister plot, 84–85
Mill on the Floss, The (Eliot): aunts in, 28, 80; familial relationships in, 80–83; sister plot in, 80; social hierarchy in, 82
Miller, Nancy, 30–31
"Mr. Harrison's Confessions" (Gaskell), 56–57
Mitchell, Margaret: *Gone with the Wind*, 13, 29
Mitchell, Juliet, 17
Moers, Ellen, 85, 88
Morrison, Toni: *Sula*, 120
Mothers, 23, 42, 108; stepmothers, 64–65, 66; surrogates, 45

Names, 43–44, 95
National Organization for Women, 19
National Women's Studies Association, 119
Neumann, Erich, 22–23
Northanger Abbey (Jane Austen), 34
Nussey, Ellen, 73–76

Olsen, Tillie, 16
Orbach, Susie, 19, 119

Patriarchy, conventions of, 21, 62, 63, 70, 75, 76, 109–10
Persuasion (Jane Austen): competition among sisters, 48–49; father in, 46–47; interchangeability of sisters, 47, 48; marriage plot, 47; portrayal of family in, 46; role splitting, 49; silences, 48–49; surrogate mother, 45
Polarization, 17–18, 20, 22, 25, 37, 85
Pollard, Arthur, 70–71
Pre-texts, nineteenth-century authors as predecessors, 21, 94–97, 112–14, 120, 122, 123–24
Pride and Prejudice (Jane Austen): alignment with father, 42–43; aunts in, 28; communication in, 44–45; emotionally significant pairs, 40; foils in, 41; rivalry in, 39–40; role splitting in, 41, 42
Psyche, 21–23, 45, 97, 126, 130
Psychologists. *See* specific names

Pym, Barbara, 98–107; *An Unsuitable Attachment*, 30, 94, 103–7; *Some Tame Gazelle*, 30, 94, 98–103. See also *Some Tame Gazelle* and *An Unsuitable Attachment*

Relationships, fluid, 26, 44
Repression, 25, 29, 56, 57–60, 72, 74
Rich, Adrienne, 21
Ricoeur, Paul, 15
Robinson, Marilynne: aunts in, 28, 121; *Housekeeping*, 14, 120, 121–22
Role splitting, 20–21, 25, 26, 27, 30; in Austen, 36–37, 39, 41, 42, 45, 49, 51, 126; in Eliot, 87–88, 89, 90, 92, 93, 126; in Gaskell, 54, 60, 75, 126; in twentieth-century works, 102, 122, 127
Rossen, Janice, 96
Rossetti, Christina, 17, 28
Rossner, Judith: *His Little Women*, 120
Rotner, Arnold, 54
Roxman, Susanna, 112

Sanditon (Jane Austen), 34
Scott, Sir Walter, 31
Sense and Sensibility (Jane Austen): conclusion of, 39; differentiation of sisters, 37, 38; interdependence in, 37; opening of, 46; rivalry in, 38; silences in, 38
Sherwood, Rhonda, 15, 102, 116
Siblings, "emotionally significant pairs," 40
Sinclair, May: *The Three Sisters*, 95
Sister (as word), 15–16, 31–32, 83, 117, 118
Sisterhood (as word), 15, 31–32
Sisterhood: idea of, 29–30, 52, 54, 60, 62, 70, 76, 77, 102; in twentieth century, 107, 116–17, 118–20, 125, 127; women's associations, 18–19, 31
Sister plot, 20–30, 34, 80, 90; revised in twentieth century, 95–97, 126–27
Sisters: biological, 14, 15–16, 28, 30, 31; differentiation of, 37; half sisters, 89, 123, 124; in authors' lives, 28, 33, 54, 78; in opposition to each other, 17–18, 20, 31, 40–41; metaphorical, 21; rivalry among, 18, 33–34, 38, 39–40, 67–68, 104; significant sister, 20. *See also* Friend-sisters; specific works

Smith-Rosenberg, Carroll, 18–19
"Snow White and Rose Red," 22
Some Tame Gazelle (Pym): compared to
    Cranford, 98–99; defensiveness in,
    101; isolation in, 100; sisterhood in
    100–101, 102; sisters' relationships,
    99, 100
Spacks, Patricia, 14, 39, 68, 69–70
Summer Bird-Cage, A (Drabble): 30, 94,
    111–17; isolation in, 113; plot tied to
    Middlemarch and *Pride and Prejudice,*
    112; sisterhood in, 116–17; sisters' re-
    lationships in, 111–14, 115

Tanner, Tony, 20, 35
Taylor, Mary, 76
Tennant, Emma, 31, 120, 123, 122–26
Thayer, Nancy: *Three Women at the
    Water's Edge,* 120
Three Sisters, The (Jane Austen), 34, 35
Training manuals, 18, 39, 55
Twinship transference, 134
Twitchell, James, 43

Unsuitable Attachment, An (Pym):
    clothing in, 103, 104–6; competition
    in, 104, 106; marriage in, 104, 107;
    revision of earlier works, 30, 94; sis-
    terhood in, 104, 107; sisters' rela-
    tionships in, 103

Venus. *See* Aphrodite

Walker, Alice: *The Color Purple,* 14, 120,
    121
Watsons, The (Jane Austen), 34
West, Rebecca: *The Fountain Overflows,*
    13, 21
Wives and Daughters (Gaskell): con-
    clusion of, 69; father in, 63–64, 65;
    rivalry between stepsisters, 67–68;
    sexuality in, 70
Woolf, Virginia, 28

Zimmerman, Bonnie, 91
Zipes, Jack, 24